Main Street Windows

Jeff Heimbuch

Printed in the United States of America
ISBN 978-0-9912954-2-5
Orchard Hill Press

DEDICATION

For Dad, whose constant inquires of "How's the book coming along?" kept me at it, even when I hit a roadblock. Thank you for your constant and unwavering support. Love you!

TABLE OF CONTENTS

FOREWORD
by Rolly Crump

I HAVE ALWAYS described Disneyland as one big salad: so many great ingredients coming together for a special experience. The Windows are a big part of that salad. Not only are the Windows indicative of Main Street, U.S.A., but, for employees of the Disney Parks, they are the Tony, the Emmy, and the Academy Award, all wrapped up in one. Each Window on Main Street is specially designed to recognize the individual and their unique contributions. They are prominent symbols recognizing people for the work they have done.

One of my earliest memories while working as Art Director of Disneyland was seeing the names on the Windows and thinking "How special is that?" My very next thought was "Only the old guys get Windows." Of course, I never dreamed I would become one of those "old guys," let alone have a window with my name on it.

I have had two honors bestowed upon me as an "old guy," and I couldn't be more proud. Receiving the Disney Legend award was very special, needless to say. But receiving a Window on Main Street was the real honor. I became one of many recognized for their part in developing the Parks into what they are today.

Having the presentation ceremony right there on Main Street was the icing on the cake. As our tour guide drove us through the Park, she casually mentioned she would take care of my Window and get it to us before we left for the day. I had no idea she meant that I would be given an exact duplicate of my Window to take home. It still hangs proudly in my living room.

Documenting the history and stories of the Windows is important, and long overdue. I can't thank Jeff enough for bringing us the stories behind the Windows: the dressing on the salad.

FOREWORD
by William "Sully" Sullivan

ONE DAY, WHILE strolling through the Magic Kingdom, I was surprised to see a Window with my name on it. The Window, for "Windermere Fraternal Hall," also included the names of some of my colleagues. It was such a special feeling to see my name up there.

I was surprised again, upon my retirement after 40 years, when they gave me my own personal Window: "Sully's Safaris & Guide Service." How honored I felt to be included with some of the greats of The Walt Disney Company.

It all started as one of Walt's many great ideas: to have something fun and interesting on the Windows on Main Street to recognize and thank the sponsors and lessees. From there, it grew into the much-loved tradition of honoring the Company's own Cast Members for their contributions to the Parks. I always thought that it was a neat way to recognize people for their hard work.

I'd like to thank Jeff for putting together such a great guide to the Windows; not just for the stateside Parks, but for the international ones as well. It's a unique idea which no one has done as thoroughly as this before. I know that everyone with their own Window would be as proud as I am. Thank you, Jeff, for all of your hard work on recognizing this part of Disney history.

Introduction

IT IS OFTEN said that Walt Disney wanted Main Street, U.S.A. to act as the opening reel for Disneyland. As you step underneath the Railroad station, the curtain is pulled back, revealing the feature presentation, allowing you to get lost in a world of yesterday, tomorrow, and fantasy.

As you walk down Main Street, U.S.A., heading toward whatever adventure lies before you, you'll find names painted on many of the Windows. Much like in a movie, the men and women whose names adorn the Windows act as the opening credits.

Nowadays, getting a Window on Main Street is a high honor. But it wasn't always that way.

The tradition dates back to before Disneyland's opening day. Many of the shops along Main Street were lessees: merchants who were renting out store space in order to sell their wares. While all of Main Street's shops are run by Disney today, back then almost everyone was an outside vendor. Renting the space from Disney allowed merchants to get prime real estate and plenty of foot traffic through their stores. On top of that, the money they paid to Disney helped to fund last-minute projects at the Park in the days leading up to the opening.

Some of the shops were not going to be ready for opening day, which led to interesting facades but empty shops. So, while the interiors were being constructed, Imagineers put a sign in the window advertising the fictitious businesses that would supposedly occupy the space. Many of these signs included the Imagineers' names as a tongue-in-cheek way to get credit for their work. Of course, since this was Disney, the signs were painted with flourish, adding to the illusion that Main Street, U.S.A. was a functional and thriving place in the heart of America.

Marty Sklar said "The tradition [of the Main Street Windows] was established by Walt Disney for Disneyland Park. He personally selected the names that would be revealed on the Main Street Windows on opening day, July 17, 1955."

As mentioned earlier, these Windows, that were apparently hand-picked by Walt, served roughly the same purpose as a screen credit on a film. They were acknowledgments given to employees for their work on the Park. Hardcore Disney fans will notice that I didn't use the term "Cast Members." That's because not every single one of these original Windows referenced people who worked for The Walt Disney Company at the time. While many did, some were contractors, hired to help get the Park ready. Some of these people only spent a handful of months working on Disneyland. However, each person who contributed to the Park in a significant way was honored by having their name prominently displayed for all to see.

To fit in with the motif of a small town at the turn of the century, the names couldn't just be painted on the window. Instead, everyone was given a whimsical, fictional business that, in many cases, related to their contribution to the Park or a hobby they enjoyed. If they were a photographer, chances are they worked for a photography company on Main Street. If they enjoyed fly fishing, then an outdoors company would be their trade. Each Window became more imaginative than the last, allowing Walt to pay tribute to those that helped him, and to breathe life into this fictional setting.

Over the past few years, the tradition of a Cast Member getting their own Window on Main Street has become a sort of lifetime achievement award. While becoming a Disney Legend is quite a feat, getting your own Window on Main Street is considered the highest honor you can achieve. Only after decades of service, and significant contributions to the Company, does a name earn a coveted place for all Guests to see. The ceremonies to present these Windows to the honorees are usually extremely personal affairs, with only a select guest list invited to share in the moment of the reveal, but the impression the Windows leaves on people lasts a lifetime.

Although the tradition of honoring people on Main Street (or, in the case of Tokyo Disneyland, World Bazaar) has gone on for years and spread to other resorts, there has never been a comprehensive list of all the Windows. While some names featured may be well known to Disney fans, there are many that may leave them scratching their heads.

In the pages that follow, you'll find a complete list (as of publication) of the Windows at all of the Magic Kingdom-style Parks in the world: Disneyland, the Magic Kingdom, Disneyland Paris, Hong Kong Disneyland, and Tokyo Disneyland. Each Window will be accompanied by a short blurb about the person it is paying tribute to.

In addition, there are some tribute Windows listed that are no longer in existence (Windows of Yesterland) and some that are not on Main Street, U.S.A. but located elsewhere in the Park (Windows Elsewhere).

How to Read This Book

The Windows in this book are presented exactly as you would see them while walking down any of the Main Streets of the world. Each section begins at the entrance to the Park, moving to the left side of Main Street and traveling toward the Castle. From there, we cross to the right side, and follow the street back to the Main Entrance.

Disneyland

FOUNDED 1955
PRICE IS RIGHT LAND COMPANY
ANAHEIM ORLANDO
CALL ON OUR NUMBERS MAN FOR THE BEST PRICE!
HARRISON "BUZZ" PRICE
FOUNDER & FINDER
WE NEVER SAY "NO"
"YES" MAKES MORE CENTS!

HARRISON "BUZZ" PRICE was not an official Disney employee, but he earned his Window by being instrumental in the development of Disneyland and Walt Disney World. Buzz was a researcher at the Stanford Research Institute, which Walt hired to help find the best location for his theme park. After advising Walt to purchase the property that eventually became Disneyland, he became one of Walt's most trusted consultants. In 1958, Buzz founded Economic Research Associates, which conducted studies pertaining to Walt Disney World and the proposed Mineral King Ski Resort.

Id Somniate Id Facite
Main Street College of Arts & Sciences
Est. 1852
Martin A. Sklar
Dean
Inspiring the Dreamers and Doers of Tomorrow

Martin A. "Marty" Sklar started working in Disneyland's publicity department before he had graduated from UCLA. He was hired to write *The Disneyland News*, a paper that was sold on Main Street. Though he returned to school in 1955, he joined Disneyland's publicity department again shortly after graduation. Marty joined WED Enterprises in 1961 to work on the attractions for the 1964-1965 New York World's Fair. He began to work closely for Walt, becoming his "unofficial" writer. Many of Walt's iconic phrases used in press releases and at public events came from Marty's pen. In 1974, Marty became Creative Lead of Imagineering, and helped develop Disney theme parks around the world for the next 35 years. He retired on July 17, 2009, on Disneyland's 54th birthday, after 54 years with the Company. "Id Somniate Id Facite" means "Dream It, Do It," which has been Marty's philosophy for years.

J.B. Lindquist
Honorary Mayor of Disneyland
"Jack of all trades
Master of fun"

Jack Lindquist was hired by Walt in 1955 as the first Advertising Manager of Disneyland. He is known for helping create some of the most memorable Disney traditions, such as the Magic Kingdom Club, Disney Dollars, the Disneyland Ambassador Program, and Grad Nite. He was promoted to Director of Marketing in 1965. He helped to set up the marketing department at Walt Disney World, and was named Vice President of Marketing for both resorts in 1972. He was given the title of President of Disneyland in 1990.

Partners Portrait Gallery
Charles Boyer
Master Illustrator

Charles Boyer started as a portrait artist at Disneyland in 1960. Within six months, he'd become the first full-time Disneyland artist, a position he would stay in for almost 40 years. He created magazine covers, advertising artwork, merchandise packaging, and more. He created the original *Partners* painting, which served as inspiration for the statue seen in Disney Parks around the world.

The Artisans Loft
Handmade Miniatures
by
Harriet Burns

Harriet Burns is often referred to as the "First Lady of Imagineering." She joined WED Enterprises in 1955 to design models for Disneyland. She helped design the look and feel of Sleeping Beauty Castle, Storybook Land Canal Boats, New Orleans Square, and more. She was pivotal in fabricating the birds for Walt Disney's Enchanted Tiki Room.

Coats & Co.
Claude Coats Proprietor
Big and Tall Sizes for Gentlemen

Claude Coats was a background artist for the animation department, working on *Snow White and the Seven Dwarfs*, *Pinocchio*, *Dumbo*, and more. He moved to WED Enterprises in 1955 to design the model for Mr. Toad's Wild Ride. He soon became a show designer, and was involved in the development of the Haunted Mansion, Pirates of the Caribbean, the Submarine Voyage, and other iconic attractions. He went on to design for almost all the Disney Parks in the world. His Window alludes to his height. Standing at over 6'6", he was a very tall man, but was known to be a gentle giant.

Elias Disney
Contractor
Est. 1895

Elias Disney was the father of Walt and Roy Disney. Though born in Canada, he moved his family to wherever he could find carpentry work. While in Chicago, he opened a contracting business in 1895. His wife, Flora, designed houses and he built them. He was a hard worker, and Walt attributed his hardworking attitude as coming from his father.

Dr. Benjamin Silverstein M.D.
General Practitioner
Have a fever? Have a flu?
Come on in and we'll cure you!

Dr. Benjamin Silverstein M.D. is not a real person. However, this Window is notable because it is one of the few located on the first floor. It alludes to the diverse nature of Main Street residents, as there is a mezuzah on the doorframe, indicating Silverstein's Jewish heritage.

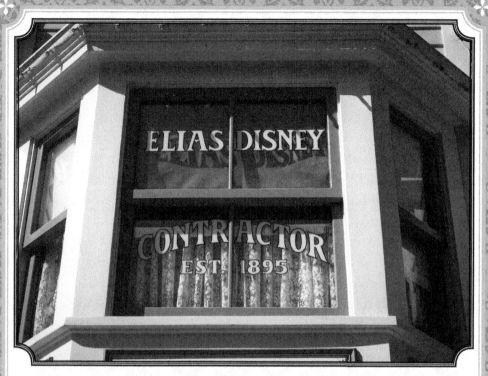

"You'll Cut A Fine Figure"
Wathel Rogers
Menswear

Wathel Rogers started as an animator at Walt Disney Studios in 1939 before moving to WED Enterprises in 1954. Because of his skill in the model shop, Wathel was asked by Walt to construct "Project Little Man," a nine-inch figure of a moving man, which was the prototype of early Audio-Animatronics. His groundbreaking achievements with the sixteenth President for Great Moments with Mr. Lincoln for the 1964-1965 New York World's Fair earned him the title of Mr. Audio-Animatronics. He spearheaded many of Imagineering's research and development projects, and became the first field art director of Walt Disney World.

Good Neighbor Foundation
"Caring and Giving Come from the Heart"
Mrs. M.A. Mang
Director

Mary Anne Mang was hired into the sales promotion department at the Disneyland Hotel after writing to Walt in 1960, asking for a job. In 1961, she moved to work in convention and tour sales. By 1972, she had become the first female manager at Disneyland when she was promoted to Public Relations Manager. She was one of the founding members of the Cast Member VoluntEARS program, and did a lot of charitable work for the American Red Cross, the American Heart Association, and the Boys and Girls Club.

"YOU'LL CUT
A
FINE FIGURE"

WATHEL ROGERS

GOOD NEIGHBOR
FOUNDATION
"Caring and Giving
Come from the Heart"
Mrs. M.A. Mang
Director

C.V. Patterson MD
W.F. Allen MD
D.S. Gilmore MD
E.G. Upjohn MD

C.V. Patterson was a senior executive at the Upjohn Company, and was not actually a doctor.

W.F. "Fred" Allen was also a senior executive at the Upjohn Company, and was not actually a doctor.

Donald S. Gilmore was Chairman and Managing Director of the Upjohn Company, and a personal friend of Walt. He was also not actually a doctor.

Dr. Everett Gifford "E.G." Upjohn was actually a doctor. He was the great-nephew of the Upjohn Company's founder, and spent his entire life working for the company. He became President of the Upjohn Company in 1953. He was a personal friend of Walt.

The Upjohn Pharmacy was located beneath these Windows when Disneyland opened in 1955.

Fine Chinese Food Restaurant

This Window is for atmosphere only, and does not pay tribute to anyone.

Main Street Gym
Christopher D. Miller
Turkish Baths
Massage Parlor

Christopher D. Miller is the oldest son of Ron Miller and Diane Disney Miller, and Walt's first grandchild. Miller worked as an assistant director on several films, such as *The Black Hole* and *Herbie Goes Bananas*.

Decorative Fountains
and Waterworks
By
Fred Joerger

Fred Joerger began his career at Disney designing backgrounds for Wathel Rogers' "Project Little Man." He went on to work with Wathel and Harriet Burns in the model shop, creating mockups for many Disneyland attractions. Fred was Disney's "resident rock expert," known for creating realistic rockwork. Though he retired in 1979, he returned as a field art director for Epcot.

Sam the Tailor

This Window is for atmosphere only, and does not pay tribute to anyone.

Old Settler's
Gold Dredging
Ed Winger
Proprietor

Ed Winger was an opening day Cast Member of Disneyland and continued to have a long career with the Park. Though he worked many jobs at the Park, he eventually became Supervisor of the Paint Department and the Mill and Sign shops. The drunken (or dead, depending on when you saw it) old settler who used to be in front of the burning cabin on Tom Sawyer Island at Disneyland was modeled after Ed, hence the first line of his Window. One of Ed's hobbies was dredging for gold, hence the second line.

Milady Fashions
Renie
Dressmaking Hemstitching & Picoting

Renie Conley was a Hollywood costume designer that Walt hired to design the costumes of Disneyland Cast Members. Renie created costumes that set the standard for costuming at all future Disney Parks. Before Disney, she worked for RKO Studios as their costume designer, and returned to the movies after working with Disney. She won an Academy Award for her costume designs for 1963's *Cleopatra*.

UNITED AUDIT
BOOKKEEPING
ACCOUNTS AUDIT
ROYAL CLARK, MGR.

ROYAL "MICKEY" CLARK was Walt Disney's personal accountant. He became Vice President and Treasurer of WED Enterprises when it was formed in 1952. Royal also became Treasurer of Retlaw Enterprises, the Disney family's private company, after Walt founded it in 1965.

FARMERS LAND CO.
REAL ESTATE AND INS.

This window is for atmosphere only, and does not pay tribute to anyone.

ACE
Insurance
Life Fire

This window is for atmosphere only, and does not pay tribute to anyone.

Theatrical Agency
Golden Vaudeville Routines
Wally Boag, Prop.

Wally Boag is most famous for playing the role of Pecos Bill for 27 years in the *Golden Horseshoe Revue*. While trying to make it in the entertainment industry, Wally was told by a friend that Disneyland was looking for actors. He auditioned, and wound up performing close to 40,000 times during his career. Walt enjoyed Wally's performances so much that he featured him in a few films and television shows, and as the voice of José in Walt Disney's Enchanted Tiki Room.

Theatrical Agency
Vaudeville Chautauqua Lyceum
Concerts, Hippodrome, Cinema

This Window is for atmosphere only, and does not pay tribute to anyone.

ABC
ABC Typing
ACME Business College
ABC Shorthand

ABC, the television network, invested $500,000 in Disneyland, and promised $4.5 million in loans. In exchange, they became one-third owners of the Park, and gained the exclusive rights to broadcast the new *Disneyland* television series, produced (and often hosted) by Walt Disney. By 1960, Disney bought back all of ABC's shares in Disneyland for $7.5 million, cutting all ties with them. However, in 1995, The Walt Disney Company bought ABC for $19 billion.

Jewelry
Diamond Gems
Wholesale only
Jewelry

This Window is for atmosphere only, and does not pay tribute to anyone.

Club 55
School of Golf
Bob Penfield
Instructor

Bob Penfield was the longest-working Cast Member of Club 55, the group of people who worked at Disneyland since 1955. Bob began his career at Disney as an attractions host for King Arthur Carrousel. After 42 years working for the Company, he retired in 1997 as a field superintendent for construction services. Bob was an avid golfer, and helped form the Club 55 golf tournament in 1990.

Alexander R. Irvine, M.D.

Dr. Alexander R. Irvine was Richard "Dick" Irvine's father. He was an ophthalmologist, and Walt's personal eye doctor. He founded the Doheny Eye Institute at the University of Southern California.

Plaza School of Art
Instructors
Herbert Ryman John Hench Peter Ellenshaw

Herbert "Herb" Ryman spent a weekend holed up with Walt in September 1953, which produced the very first defining image of Disneyland. Herb was an amazing concept illustrator, and his work helped shape the look of Sleeping Beauty Castle, Main Street, Frontierland, Tomorrowland, and more at Disneyland. He went on to create iconic concept sketches of the Magic Kingdom, Epcot, and Tokyo Disneyland, even after he officially retired in 1971. When he passed away in 1989, he was working on sketches for Disneyland Paris.

John Hench began his career at Disney in 1939 as a sketch artist on *Fantasia*. He worked in many areas of the Studios before moving to WED Enterprises in 1954 to work on Tomorrowland. From there, he helped design attractions for the Park and for the 1964-1965 New York World's Fair. After Walt's passing, John went on to play a pivotal role in the master plan and design of Walt Disney World. As Senior Vice President of Imagineering, he contributed concepts for Tokyo Disneyland, Disney's Animal Kingdom, Tokyo DisneySea, Disney California Adventure, and Hong Kong Disneyland. He continued working in Imagineering up until his death in 2004, and was the longest-serving Disney employee, having been with the Company for 65 years. In addition, he was also Mickey Mouse's official portrait artist from 1953 to 2003. He was a true renaissance man, having worked as an artist, storyteller, and color designer.

Peter Ellenshaw began working for Disney in 1948 as a matte painter, while they were filming in England for *Treasure Island*. He moved to California in 1952 to work on *20,000 Leagues Under The Sea*. He continued to do matte paintings for many Disney films, including *Mary Poppins*, for which he won an Academy Award. Peter was responsible for creating the iconic illustration of Disneyland that Walt used on his television show. Peter added blacklight paint to it, to see how the Park would look during evening hours.

CARTOGRAPHY
MASTERWORKS
SAM McKIM
MAP MAKER TO THE KINGDOM
THERE'S MAGIC IN THE DETAILS

SAM McKIM was a former child actor who started to work for WED Enterprises in 1954. He painted amazing, inspirational concept sketches for The Golden Horseshoe Saloon, Carousel of Progress, the Haunted Mansion, and more. He is probably best known for his Disneyland souvenir maps, which were sold between 1958 and 1964. Although he retired in 1987, he returned in 1992 to create a souvenir map for Disneyland Paris.

KINGDOM PHOTO SERVICES
"MAGIC EYE TO THE WORLD"
RENIE BARDEAU
PHOTOGRAPHER ARCHIVIST

RENIE BARDEAU was a photo archivist and Chief Photographer of Disneyland for almost 40 years. He started in 1959, after spending 5 years in the US Navy as an aviation photographer. As there were no internships available at the *Los Angeles Herald-Examiner*, Renie took a summer photography job at Disneyland. He became full time in 1964, and earned the title of Chief Photographer in 1975. During his time, he took over a million photos, including the iconic image of Walt Disney walking through Sleeping Beauty Castle during an early morning. He retired in 1998.

Ambassador Finishing School
Cicely Rigdon
Instructor

Cicely Rigdon tried to get a job at Disneyland four times before successfully getting hired as a ticket seller in 1957. In 1959, she became a tour guide, and helped to develop that department by leaps and bounds. By 1967, she had become Supervisor of Guest Relations, including being "Keeper of the Keys," responsible for maintaining Walt's apartment above the Firehouse. In 1982, she took over the Disneyland Ambassador Program, where she worked with thirteen ambassadors before retiring in 1994.

The Disneyland News
Edward T. Meck
Editor in Chief

Edward "Eddie" T. Meck became the first Chief of Publicity for Disneyland in March 1955, after spending over 30 years as an entertainment publicist. Eddie was responsible for the first Disneyland press event, which invited journalists to experience the Park for themselves. He did such a good job of promoting the opening day that huge crowds of people, most with counterfeit tickets, showed up on that "Black Sunday." Eddie was in charge of *The Disneyland News*, the paper sold on Main Street, which is notable for giving Marty Sklar his first job at Disney. Eddie helped to form the publicity department for Walt Disney World before retiring in 1972.

FARGO'S PALM PARLOR
PREDICATIONS THAT WILL HAUNT YOU
BAZAAR, WHIMSICAL & WEIRD
DESIGNS TO DIE FOR
ROLAND F. CRUMP
ASSISTANT TO THE PALM READER

ROLAND "ROLLY" FARGO CRUMP JR. joined the animation department in 1952 and worked on such classic films as *Peter Pan*, *Lady and the Tramp*, and *101 Dalmatians*. He moved to WED Enterprises in 1959 and worked on attractions, such as the Haunted Mansion, Walt Disney's Enchanted Tiki Room, and "it's a small world." Though he left WED in 1970, he continued to come back over the years to work on projects for the Magic Kingdom and Epcot. Rolly's Window pays tribute to many of his works, including the Adventureland Bazaar and the never-built Museum of the Weird. He is "Assistant to the Palm Reader" because he used to bring people to John Hench to have their palms read.

His is one of two Disneyland Windows that have a corresponding sign beneath it, with his reading "Fargo's Palm Parlor."

YESMEN
ENGINEERING ASSOCIATES
NO CHALLENGE TOO BIG FOR OUR YES MEN!
WE KNOW NO "NO"
DON EDGREN
CHIEF ENGINEER

DON EDGREN worked at Disneyland in its very early stages. As one of the engineers for Wheeler & Gray, the engineering firm in charge of the structural design of the Park, Don became Chief Engineer onsite in 1954. He worked for Wheeler & Gray until being hired by WED Enterprises in 1961, where he went on to work on attractions for the 1964-1965 New York World's Fair and Disneyland. He was Head of Field Engineering for Walt Disney World during its construction, and Director of Engineering for Tokyo Disneyland. He was known for saying "yes" to every challenge thrown his way, which is why he knows no "No."

PHOTOGRAPHIC STUDIO
"BRIGHT VIEWS TO ORDER"
C. "RANDY" BRIGHT
PROPRIETOR

C. RANDY BRIGHT was one of the first Cast Members to work on the Sailing Ship Columbia. From there, he worked on virtually every attraction within the Park, and also as a costumed character. He moved to Disney University in 1965, where he created presentations. In 1968, he became a writer at WED Enterprises, and then Director of Scripts and Show Development, and Vice President of Concept Development. He helped with scripts for film projects in nearly every Disney theme park, including Disneyland, Epcot, and Tokyo Disneyland. He wrote the book *Disneyland: Inside Story*. He was an avid photographer in his spare time. The Camera Center used to be located below his Window, until it was moved in the 1990s.

H. Draegert Barnard
Real Estate
Houses Bought and Sold

Dr. Harold Draegert Barnard was an eye, ear, and throat specialist who began practicing in California in 1922. He was also Walt Disney's doctor. Though he didn't actually do real estate, his Window refers to the fact that he secretly helped Walt acquire some of the property that would eventually become Disneyland.

Global Exports and Expats
Specializing in Land & Sea Operations
Our Motto:
"The Sun Never Sets on our Magical Kingdoms"
Jim Cora
Master Operator

Jim Cora started as a part-time Cast Member in 1958, and climbed through the ranks in no time at all. He helped open Walt Disney World in 1971, and then came back to Disneyland in 1974 to become Director of Operations for Fantasyland and Tomorrowland. He helped with management duties at Tokyo Disneyland before working on the plan for Disneyland Paris. He was made President of Disneyland International in 1995, and then took over as Chairman in 1999. His experiences with Tokyo Disneyland and Tokyo DisneySea earned him the "Land & Sea" portion of his Window.

Leading the Race to the Future
Meteor Cycle Co.
Our vehicles pass the test of time
Fast Faultless and Fadless
Bob Gurr
Design Impresario

Bob Gurr was hired out of art school to consult on the design of the Autopia cars. What followed was a career that spanned almost four decades. He has developed over 100 designs for all sorts of vehicles, from the Matterhorn Bobsleds, the Monorail, to the vehicles on Main Street, and more. If it is on wheels at Disneyland, chances are that Bob designed it. Though he had no formal training in engineering, Bob took it upon himself to learn, and his skills are unsurpassed.

His is one of two Disneyland Windows that have a corresponding sign beneath it, with his reading "Meteor Cycle Co."

Piano Lessons
Ask For Sara
Upstairs

This Window is for atmosphere only, and does not pay tribute to anyone. However, every so often you can hear someone practicing piano from the Window.

E.S. Bitz, D.D.S.
Licensed to Use Laughing Gas
Dentists in Training

E.S. Bitz is not a real person. It is often claimed that the "E.S." is a reference to Eddie Sotto, but according to Sotto himself, that is simply not true. However, every so often you can hear the sounds of the dentist's office from the Window.

New Century
Character Company
Custom Character Design and
Parade Illuminations
Bill Justice
Master Delineator

BILL JUSTICE first joined The Walt Disney Company as an animator in 1937, where he worked on such classics as *Alice in Wonderland*, *Fantasia*, and *Peter Pan*. He joined WED Enterprises in 1965 at the behest of Walt. He programmed many of the Audio-Animatronic figures for Mission to Mars, Pirates of the Caribbean, Great Moments with Mr. Lincoln, and more. He was also involved in creating the spectacular costumes used in many of the Disneyland parades, including the very first Disneyland Christmas parade and the Main Street Electrical Parade.

Detective Agency
"We Never Sleep"
W. Dennis Cottrell
Private Investigator

WILLIAM H.D. "BILL" COTTRELL joined Walt Disney Studios in 1929 as a cameraman, and worked as an animation short director before moving over to the story department. He worked on *Pinocchio*, *Saludos Amigos*, and *Peter Pan*. Bill was one of the first ever Imagineers, holding the title of Vice President, and later President, of WED Enterprises. He developed the handbook that helps Cast Members refer to every attraction and area of the Park by the correct name. Bill married into the Disney family when he wed Hazel Sewell, Lillian's sister. He became The Walt Disney Company's first 50-year employee in 1979. Bill was very passionate about Sherlock Holmes, hence the reference to a "Detective Agency" and a "Private Investigator" on his Window.

The PICO Organization
Installation & Coordination of World Class Projects
"We Never Sleep – In Any Time Zone"
Orlando Ferrante
Founder

Orlando Ferrante was a 40-year veteran of The Walt Disney Company, having overseen the engineering, design production, and installation of Disney Parks all around the world. After playing football during college with Disney employees Dick Nunis and Ron Miller, Orlando joined the Company in 1962. He helped with such projects as Walt Disney's Enchanted Tiki Room, Great Moments with Mr. Lincoln, and Carousel of Progress. He formed PICO (Project Installation Coordinating Office). He retired with the title of Vice President of Engineering, Design and Production.

Buena Vista Construction Co.
Jack Rorex
Ivan Martin
Cash Shockey

Buena Vista Construction Company is where Walt Disney Studios was located at the time of the Park's construction, on Buena Vista Street in Burbank. However, a real company with this name was founded when The Walt Disney Company began building Walt Disney World. The company still exists today.

Jack Rorex was Head of Construction for Walt Disney Studios, which provided the sets for the Park. He also supervised the construction of sets for *20,000 Leagues Under The Sea*.

Ivan Martin worked under Jack Rorex in construction. He was an expert prop maker for Walt Disney Studios.

Cash Shockey was a set painter, in charge of the paint department at Walt Disney Studios. He oversaw all of the painting work done at Disneyland.

ROBERT WASHO
STONE MASON

ROBERT "BUD" WASHO was a senior designer for WED Enterprises. He also headed the staff shop, which created all of the concrete and plastic work for Disneyland, from 1955 until 1967. Later in his career, he was Manager of Architectural Ornamentation for Epcot's World Showcase. For years, the Window mistakenly featured the name "Robert Wisky," until it was corrected in 2008.

SEB MOREY
TAXIDERMIST

SEBASTIAN MORENO, whose nickname is "Seb Morey," began working for Disney in 1955, and was a decorator and supervisor for 38 years. However, he was never a taxidermist. The Window originally read "Bob Mattey – Taxidermist" before the name and location of the Window changed.

BOB MATTEY created many of the special effects for Disney films, including *20,000 Leagues Under The Sea*, and *Mary Poppins*. He designed the movements of the animals on the Jungle Cruise, which meant the title of "Taxidermist" made more sense for his Window.

WAX
BEE
KEEPERS
SUPPLIES

This Window is for atmosphere only, and does not pay tribute to anyone.

GEO. WHITNEY
GUNS

GEORGE WHITNEY JR. ran Playland, an amusement park in San Francisco, with his father and uncle, before Disneyland existed. Walt hired him as Director of Ride Operations because he had experience running an amusement park. Aside from being an attractions manager in Fantasyland, George designed the shooting galleries in Adventureland and Frontierland. He was the seventh Disneyland employee.

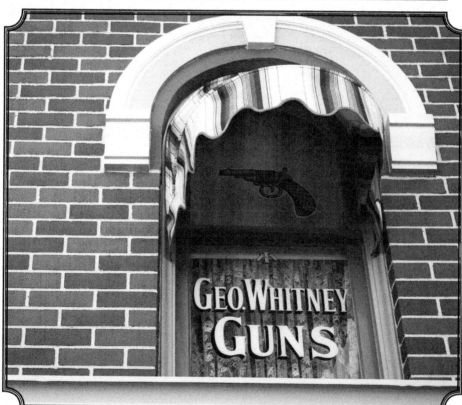

Royal Care Co.
We Keep Your Castle Shining
Chuck Boyajian
Prop.

Chuck Boyajian was the very first Custodial Manager at Disneyland, after being given the position by Walt himself in 1955. Chuck set a standard never before seen in outdoor themed entertainment, firmly believing that "cleanliness breeds cleanliness." Chuck's policies and procedures set guidelines for all future Disney Parks. He moved to Florida in 1971 to head the custodial department there, and retired in 1981. He came back to work in 1982 to help set up Tokyo Disneyland's custodial department.

Emile Kuri
Interior Decorator

Emile Kuri joined Walt Disney Studios in 1952 as Chief Decorator for such films as *The Parent Trap*, *Mary Poppins*, and *20,000 Leagues Under The Sea*, for which he won an Academy Award. Emile's keen sense of style made him instrumental in the design of Disneyland, where he was the primary decorator for Walt's apartment above the Firehouse, the shops on Main Street, Club 33, and much more. He supervised the Disney exhibits at the 1964-65 New York World's Fair. Later, he was a design consultant for the Magic Kingdom. Emile retired in 1974.

ORANGE GROVE
PROPERTY MGT.
"WE'LL CARE FOR YOUR PROPERTY
AS IF IT WERE OUR OWN"
RON DOMINGUEZ
OWNER

RON DOMINGUEZ had a place at Disneyland well before the Park opened in 1955. His family owned ten acres of Anaheim orange groves that Walt Disney purchased. That property eventually became part of Disneyland. Ron's childhood home originally stood where Pirates of the Caribbean is today. The house was moved behind Main Street and, for years, was used as administrative offices for the Park. The Canary Island Date Palm tree that sits between the Jungle Cruise and Indiana Jones Adventure also belonged to Ron's family. Ron began working for Disneyland in 1955 as a ticket taker, before moving on to portray Davy Crockett on the Mike Fink Keel Boats for a few years. Eventually, he moved his way up through the ranks to become Executive Vice President of Walt Disney Attractions. He retired in 1994 after 39 years with the Company.

CARPENTERS & JOINERS
GEORGE MILLS
RAY CONWAY
CHAS. ALEXANDER

GEORGE MILLS was Foreman of the Disneyland Construction Department's Mill, where all of the lumber used for building Disneyland was cut and prepared. The Mill itself was constructed onsite in 1954, in the Opera House.

RAY CONWAY was in charge of all the construction at Disneyland.

CHARLES ALEXANDER was Field Supervisor for the Disneyland Construction Department.

The three men worked closely to make sure Disneyland was ready for opening day. The Window originally had a line saying "Carpenters & Joiners," to further explain their significance to the Park.

CARPENTERS & JOINERS
SURVEYING & ENGINEERING
L.H. ROTH

LOU ROTH helped coordinate labor, to make sure Disneyland opened on July 17, 1955. He was Admiral Joe Fowler's assistant.

SHIP MODELS
BUSHMAN & DAGRADI
MFGS.

BRUCE BUSHMAN joined Walt Disney Studios as a layout artist in the late 1930s, and worked on *Pinocchio* and several shorts. He was also an art director for the *Nutcracker Suite* segment of *Fantasia*. He helped to design many of the Fantasyland attractions, such as Dumbo the Flying Elephant, Casey Jr. Circus Train and Mad Tea Party. He also acquired many of the hand-carved horses for King Arthur Carrousel. Bushman left soon after Disneyland opened, to work as a layout artist for television animation.

DON DAGRADI began his Disney career as a layout artist in 1937, but soon became an art director for *Dumbo*. Eventually, he became a story man as well, when he co-wrote *Mary Poppins*, *The Love Bug*, and many more. He worked on Disneyland in the 1950s, helping to design some of the Fantasyland attractions, such as Mr. Toad's Wild Ride.

KEN ANDERSON
BAIT CO.

KEN ANDERSON began his career at Disney in 1934, and worked on the *Silly Symphonies* before becoming art director on *Snow White and the Seven Dwarfs*. He wrote for many other classic Disney films, such as *The Jungle Book* and *Robin Hood*. In the 1950s, Anderson moved to WED Enterprises, and became the art director for many of the Fantasyland attractions, and contributed concepts for other rides, such as the Haunted Mansion. Though he retired in 1978, he still developed designs for special projects, such as Epcot. Anderson was a fly fisherman, and Walt honored him with this Window as a joke, since fly fisherman do not use live bait.

Youngman & Leopold
Gunther R Lessing Esq.

GORDON YOUNGMAN was a senior partner at the law firm Youngman, Hungate and Leopold, which was hired by Gunther Lessing to oversee all legal affairs at Disneyland. Youngman also served on the Disney Board of Directors.

FREDERIC LEOPOLD was also a senior partner in the law firm of Youngman, Hungate and Leopold when they were hired by Gunther Lessing. Leopold was Mayor of Beverly Hills, elected in 1967 and 1971. The name of the firm changed to Leopold, Petrich and Smith in 1984.

GUNTHER R. LESSING was hired by Walt Disney, shortly after Walt lost the rights to Oswald the Lucky Rabbit, to help protect his newest endeavors. He became Head of the Legal Department at Walt Disney Studios, and eventually Vice President and General Counsel. He was a member of the Board of Directors for Walt Disney Productions from 1938 until his retirement in 1964. Walt often said that "the only Mister we have at the Studio is our lawyer, Mr. Lessing."

Far East Imports
Exotic Art
Marc Davis
Proprietor

Marc Davis was one of Walt's famous "Nine Old Men." He was instrumental in helping Walt establish his place in animation history, and was responsible for developing such characters as Cinderella and Tinker Bell. In 1961, after working on *101 Dalmatians*, Walt asked Davis to move over to WED Enterprises, to help develop story concepts, character designs, and gags for some of the Disneyland attractions. His sketches for the Haunted Mansion, Pirates of the Caribbean, and the Jungle Cruise are some of the most well-known concept art in the Disney world. Though he retired in 1978, he continued to contribute designs for Epcot and Tokyo Disneyland. His Window alludes to his large collection of New Guinea art.

Small World Costume Co.
Alice Davis
Seamstress to the Stars

Alice Davis took a class taught by Disney animator Marc Davis at the Chouinard Art Institute in 1947. After launching her own career designing women's lingerie years later, Marc called her to see if she would be interested in designing costumes for live-action reference for *Sleeping Beauty*. This led not only to a long career at Disney, but also to her marriage to Marc in 1956. In 1963, Davis officially joined WED Enterprises to design over 150 costumes for "it's a small world" for the 1964-65 New York World's Fair. After that, she went on to design costumes for many other classic Disney attractions, such as Pirates of the Caribbean. She retired from the Company in 1978.

OPERATING IN MANY LANDS AROUND THE WORLD
THE CAST DOCTOR
CELEBRATING OUR 50TH
"EVERY CAST A PERFECT FIT"
GREG A. EMMER
SPECIALIZING IN CASTING SINCE '68

GREG A. EMMER started in 1968, working as a ride operator on Matterhorn Bobsleds during his college years. After graduation, he was promoted to management, and he later moved to Florida to assist in opening Walt Disney World. He continued to move up the chain, becoming Senior Vice President of Disneyland Resort Operations in 2003. It was in this role that he supervised preparations for the Disneyland 50th Anniversary celebration in 2005. He retired in 2008.

OPEN SINCE '55
DISNEYLAND
CASTING AGENCY
"IT TAKES PEOPLE TO MAKE THE DREAM A REALITY"
WALTER ELIAS DISNEY
FOUNDER & DIRECTOR EMERITUS

WALTER ELIAS DISNEY is the name on this Window, although it is actually a tribute to all Disneyland Resort Cast Members, past and present.

Van Arsdale France
Founder and Professor Emeritus
Disney Universities

Van Arsdale France was hired in March 1955, and had a number of jobs for the Company. He is best known for the creation of Disney University, where he taught Cast Members new concepts in Guest Relations. He used Walt Disney's philosophies to teach new hires how to be "Ambassadors of Happiness." Upon his retirement in 1978, he helped found the Disneyland Alumni Club for former Cast Members. France was known to be a chain smoker, so his Window was placed above the Tobacco Shop (now the home of 20th Century Music Company).

Van Arsdale
Station

Founder
and
Professor Emeritus
Disney Universities

Two Brothers
Tunemakers
Richard M. Sherman and
Robert B. Sherman
Proprietors
"We'll write your tunes for a song!"

Richard M. Sherman and Robert B. Sherman are better known collectively as the Sherman Brothers. They became Walt Disney Studios' staff songwriters in 1960 after writing a number of hit songs for Mouseketeer Annette Funicello. The Sherman Brothers wrote over 200 songs for Disney films and television shows, including their Academy Award-winning score for *Mary Poppins*. They also continued to write songs for Disney attractions, such as the classic songs *It's a Small World*, *The Tiki Tiki Tiki Room*, and *There's a Great Big Beautiful Tomorrow*. Both Shermans retired in 1973, but continued to contribute music to the Disney Parks until Robert's passing in 2012.

Main Street Marvels
Tony Baxter
Inventor
Imagination is at the heart of our Creations

Tony Baxter started his career at Disney in 1965, serving ice cream at Carnation Plaza Gardens. He went on to work in the Parks for five years in various roles until he joined Imagineering in 1970. Tony played a key role in many of the modern-day attractions, such as Big Thunder Mountain Railroad, Indiana Jones Adventure, Star Tours, and Splash Mountain, and also helped to update some classics such as Great Moments with Mr. Lincoln. He was made Senior Vice President of Imagineering, and made significant contributions for Disneyland Paris during its inception. He held that title until he retired in 2013.

"Can Do"
Machine Works
Mechanical Wonders
Live Steam Engines
Magical Illusions
Cameras
Roger Broggie
Shopmaster
"Advisor to the Magic Makers"

ROGER E. BROGGIE is often considered to be the first Imagineer (aside from Walt) to work for WED Enterprises. Broggie joined the Studio in 1939 as a precision machinist. Installing the multi-plane camera was one of his first assignments. Once Walt learned Broggie was an avid railroad fan, he asked him to help design the layout of the Carolwood Pacific Railroad, which ran around Walt's Holmby Hills home. He also helped create the Lilly Belle, the miniature steam engine. In 1950, Broggie was promoted to Head of the Machine Shop, and created Academy Award-winning effects, such as the ones used in *20,000 Leagues Under The Sea*. In 1951, he and Wathel Rogers worked on "Project Little Man," which was a forerunner of Audio-Animatronics. Broggie went on to work on such attractions as the Disneyland Railroad, the Monorail, and the first life-size human Audio-Animatronic figure, Abraham Lincoln. Broggie retired in 1975, and shortly after, one of the locomotives at the Magic Kingdom was named after him. "Can Do" was a phrase Broggie was known for saying whenever something was asked of him.

HAPPIEST DREAMS ON EARTH
INTERNATIONAL SCHOOL OF HOSPITALITY
HIDEO AMEMIYA
HEADMASTER
"WE PUT PEOPLE FIRST"

HIDEO AMEMIYA started with The Walt Disney Company in 1971 at the Polynesian Resort, where he used his experience in hotel management to help integrate Disney's service philosophies. He served as Director of Resort Operations until he was reassigned to Tokyo Disneyland. After that, he became Vice President and General Manager of the Disneyland Hotels, before being promoted to Senior Vice President of Disneyland Resort Hotels in 2000. He managed the opening of Disney's Grand Californian Hotel & Spa and the transition of the Disney Pacific Hotel into Disney's Paradise Pier Hotel.

COAST TO COAST PEOPLEMOVING
WORLD LEADER IN LEISURE MANAGEMENT
DICK NUNIS
PROPRIETOR
FOUNDED 1955
OFFICES
ANAHEIM ORLANDO TOKYO
WAVE MACHINES A SPECIALTY

RICHARD "DICK" NUNIS was hired in 1955 by Van Arsdale France to help with training Disneyland employees. Soon after, he was promoted to Attractions Supervisor, where he was responsible for developing the standard operating procedures for the Disneyland attractions. Later, as Chairman of the Park Operations Committee, he was instrumental in helping get the Florida Project off the ground. He was promoted to Executive Vice President of Walt Disney World and Disneyland in 1971, and served as member of the Board of Directors from 1981 to 1999. "Coast to Coast Peoplemoving" refers to how Nunis convinced many of the Disneyland Cast Members to move to Florida to help open Walt Disney World. "Wave Machines a Specialty" is an inside joke, referring to Nunis' love of surfing. While he was President of Disney's Outdoor Recreation Division, he had a wave machine installed in Seven Seas Lagoon, so he (and Guests) could surf. Unfortunately, it was eroding away the shoreline, and had to be turned off for good.

John Louis Catone
Locksmith

John Louis Catone was originally from Ohio, but he left for California after learning that Disney was hiring for its new Park. He began work on opening day, as an Autopia operator. He was also one of the iconic spacemen that walked around Tomorrowland. Catone later became Manager of Communication Services for Disneyland, quite literally being the one to hold the "Keys to the Kingdom," hence his position as a locksmith on his Window.

Ragin' Ray's
River Rafting Expeditions
Experienced Guides since '55
Ray Van De Warker
Owner Guide

Ray Van De Warker applied for a summer job at Disneyland before it opened in 1955. He originally worked on King Arthur Carrousel and was one of the first Tom Sawyer Island raft drivers. He unknowingly helped create a Disneyland tradition when he was in charge of the Davy Crockett Explorer Canoes. In 1963, Bob Penfield, who was in charge at the Jungle Cruise, suggested the two crews compete in a canoe race around the Rivers of America. Van de Warker's canoe crew won, and an annual tradition was born. He retired in 1996 as Manager of Office Support Systems.

The Musical Quill
Lyrics and Librettos
By X. Atencio

Francis Xavier "X" Atencio joined Disney as an inbetweener on *Fantasia* in 1938. He was promoted to Assistant Animator within three years, before enlisting in the US Army Air Corps in 1941. He served until 1945, earning the rank of Captain, before returning to Walt Disney Studios. Atencio continued to work as an animator until 1965, when he moved over to WED Enterprises. His first assignment was to work on the design of the Primeval World Diorama for the Disneyland Railroad. After that, Walt asked him to write the dialogue and lyrics for two of their latest attractions. Atencio had never written before, but he was able to pen two of the most famous Disney attraction songs of all time: *Yo Ho (A Pirate's Life For Me)* with composer George Bruns, and *Grim Grinning Ghosts* with composer Buddy Baker. Atencio went on to become the in-house scriptwriter for many of the attractions that WED developed.

MILT ALBRIGHT
ENTREPRENEUR
NO JOB TOO BIG
NO JOB TOO SMALL

MILT ALBRIGHT started as a junior accountant at Walt Disney Studios in 1947. However, in 1953, he tried to impress Walt by designing a mini-car ride for the Disneyland project. Walt saw Albright's talent, and hired him as Manager of Accounting for Disneyland. This earned him the title of Disneyland's first official employee. Albright went on to become Manager of Marketing Special Projects, where he helped create the Magic Kingdom Club in 1958 and Disneyland's Grad Nite in 1961. He retired in 1992, as Manager of Guest Communications.

THE BUSY HANDS SCHOOL
SCULPTING, WHITTLING & SOAP CARVING
BLAINE GIBSON
HEADMASTER
THE ETERNAL PURSUIT OF THE ARTISTS CRAFT

BLAINE GIBSON joined Walt Disney Studios in 1939 as an animator. For years, he worked on classic animated Disney films, before going home to sculpt models as a hobby. Walt saw some of his sculptures, and recruited him to work for WED Enterprises. Blaine became Head of the Sculpture Studio at WED, and helped create some of the memorable figures you now see at Disney Parks worldwide, from pirates to presidents. Blaine retired in 1983, but came back to work on special projects, such as the *Partners* statue seen at the Disney Studio, Disneyland, Walt Disney World, Tokyo Disneyland and Disneyland Paris. "Soap Carving" refers to Blaine's childhood hobby of sculpting miniatures out of bars of soap.

Evans Gardens
Exotic & Rare Species
Freeway Collections
Est. 1910
Morgan (Bill) Evans
Senior Partner

Morgan "Bill" Evans was hired to landscape Walt Disney's Holmby Hills home in the early 1950s. Walt liked his work so much that he hired Bill and his brother, Jack, to landscape Disneyland. Eventually, Bill became Director of Landscape Design for WED Enterprises. Even after he retired in 1975, Bill stayed on as a consultant for many Disney theme parks, such as Epcot, Tokyo Disneyland, and Disney's Animal Kingdom. "Exotic & Rare" alludes to the Evans-Reeves Landscaping & Nursery business that Bill used to run, known for its rare and exotic plants. "Freeway Collections" refers to how he found trees for Disneyland amongst Southern California's freeway construction, and had them transplanted to the Park.

World Headquarters
Main Street Electrical Parade
Robert F. Jani
Master Showman

Robert F. "Bob" Jani started at Disneyland in 1955 as Director of Guest Relations at the age of 21. Though he left to form his own company in 1961, he returned in 1967 as Director of Entertainment. He was appointed Vice President of Entertainment in 1972 for both Disneyland and Walt Disney World, and helped produced some of the Park's most memorable parades, such as America on Parade and the much-loved Main Street Electrical Parade.

WADE B. RUBOTTOM
GEORGE PATRICK

WADE B. RUBOTTOM worked as Art Director for Main Street, and helped enhance its overall look. Previously, he worked for Metro-Goldwyn-Mayer Studios doing the same, working on such films as *The Wizard of Oz*. He left Disney shortly after the Park opened in 1955, and went on to help create Freedomland, a short-lived theme park in the Bronx about the history of the United States.

GEORGE PATRICK served as Art Designer for Frontierland in 1954. He left after the Park opened, and went on to provide art direction for numerous films and television shows.

ARCHITECTS AND ASSOCIATES
WILSON MARTIN
GABRIEL SCOGNAMILLO

WILSON "BILL" MARTIN joined WED Enterprises in 1953 as an art director and project designer for such Disneyland attractions as Snow White's Scary Adventures, Peter Pan's Flight, Carnation Plaza Gardens, and Mine Train Through Nature's Wonderland. He also created the master layout for the Magic Kingdom, including the Utilidor system, and helped with the design of Cinderella Castle. He also designed various watercraft for the resort, such as the Admiral Joe Fowler and Richard F. Irvine riverboats used in Seven Seas Lagoon. Later, Martin did the master plan and overall layout for Tokyo Disneyland. Before he retired in 1977, he was the architectural designer for the Italy and Mexico pavilions at Epcot.

GABRIEL SCOGNAMILLO was an Academy Award-nominated art director who started at WED Enterprises in 1954. He was in charge of the design for Tomorrowland, and he left the Company shortly after the Park opened.

RICHARD IRVINE
MARVIN DAVIS

RICHARD F. "DICK" IRVINE was hired by Walt Disney in 1952 to act as liaison between Walt Disney Productions and the architectural firm that was being considered to build Disneyland. Formerly an art director at 20th Century Fox, Irvine had worked with Disney in the past, but never in this capacity. Over time, he realized that the best people to build the Park were Walt's own staff. So, he headed up design and planning for all of Disneyland's attractions himself. He continued to stay in this role once the Park opened. During the early 1960s, he supervised the attractions that Disney was building for the 1964-65 New York World's Fair. In 1967, Irvine was appointed Vice President and Chief Operations Officer of WED Enterprises. He helped develop the master plan for Walt Disney World, and continued to oversee Disney attractions until retiring in 1973.

MARVIN DAVIS was recruited by Richard Irvine in 1953 to help with the design of Disneyland. Davis had worked with Irvine as an art director at 20th Century Fox, and was perfect for the task. Davis became Master Planner for Disneyland, and helped to lay out almost every inch of the Park. After the Park opened in 1955, Davis became an art director for some of Disney's films and television shows. He won an Emmy in 1962 for an episode of *Walt Disney's Wonderful World of Color*. He returned to WED Enterprises in 1965 as a project designer for Walt Disney World. He helped to design some of its original hotels, such as the Polynesian Resort and the Contemporary. Davis married Walt's niece, Marjorie Sewell. After 22 years with the Company, he retired in 1975.

Seven Summits Expeditions
Frank G. Wells
President
"For Those Who Want To Do It All"

Frank G. Wells was The Walt Disney Company's President and Chief Operating Officer, beginning in 1984. He worked closely with Chairman and Chief Executive Officer Michael Eisner to help stabilize The Walt Disney Company when it was in rough shape. Together, they restored Disney's name and image to its former glory, and helped raise its profit margin by over $7 billion in ten years. Wells was a very hands-on President, and oversaw much of the Company's daily operations. He was an avid adventurer, and it was his goal to scale the seven continents' tallest peaks. He was able to accomplish all but one, Mount Everest, which he attempted twice. He passed away in a helicopter crash in 1994. "Seven Summits Expeditions" honors his goal of trying to reach all the summits.

J.S. Hamel
Consulting Engineer

Jacob Samuel Hamel was hired as a civil and electric consultant for Disneyland after being recommended by General Electric. Hamel was tasked with taking the concept drawings by Imagineers and turning them into structurally sound, working buildings. He was also responsible for the lighting of Disneyland, along with creating the system of waterways that flows around the Park. With the help of Admiral Joe Fowler, Hamel designed the Submarine Voyage. Later, Hamel became a lighting consultant for Walt Disney World.

William T. Wheeler
John Wise
Structural Engineers

William T. Wheeler was the co-founder of Wheeler & Gray, the firm hired as engineering consultants for Disneyland's construction. Wheeler was born in Oklahoma, and his family moved to California in 1922, where he went to the California Institute of Technology to earn a Civil Engineering degree. In 1946, he co-founded Wheeler & Gray Consulting Engineers. Imagineers Don Edgren and John Wise both originally worked for Wheeler & Gray before being hired by WED Enterprises. William Wheeler continued to run the company until his death in October 2000. The firm continues to consult on Disney's projects to this day.

John Wise was originally employed by Wheeler & Gray before working in several engineering positions for WED Enterprises and the Buena Vista Construction Company. Eventually, he became Chief Engineer of Disneyland. In 1974, he was the first President of the Community Transportation Division of Walt Disney Productions.

WINDOWS ELSEWHERE

TEXAS GLENN'S
HONEY BEE FARM
"OUR BEES ARE REAL HUMMERS"
GLENN HICKS
PROPRIETOR

GLENN "SLIPPERY" HICKS was Director of New Orleans Square, Bear Country, Adventureland, and Frontierland. He coached the Company's baseball team for years, and led them to victory many times. He was a member of The *Order of the Red Handkerchief*, a club for Cast Members who worked on Mine Train Through Nature's Wonderland at Disneyland. His Window, which can be found at Bonanza Outfitters in Frontierland, alludes to his hobby, and later full-time job, as a beekeeper. He sold honey under the name "Texas Glenn's Honey."

DAVY CROCKETT
COONSKIN CAP SUPPLY CO.
FESS PARKER
PROPRIETOR

FESS PARKER was hired in 1954 to play Davy Crockett on television, and was the first adult performer to be put under a long-term contract by Walt Disney Studios. The show was extremely popular, leading to the theme song (sung by Parker himself) reaching the Billboard top ten in 1955. Coonskin caps, as worn by Davy, were major sellers at Disneyland. Fess would go on to star in other films for Disney, including *The Great Locomotive Chase* and *Old Yeller*. In his later years, he developed and operated the Fess Parker Family Winery & Vineyard in Los Olivos, California. His Window can be found at Pioneer Mercantile in Frontierland.

Oriental Tattooing
By Prof. Harper Goff
Banjo Lessons

Ralph Harper Goff was originally hired to sketch concepts for *20,000 Leagues Under The Sea* before moving over to WED Enterprises. Harper helped to design much of Disneyland during his time there, including as Lead Designer for Adventureland, where his Window is located (next to the Bazaar). He helped shape how Main Street looked, based on Marceline, Missouri and his hometown of Fort Collins, Colorado. An avid banjo player, as his Window alludes, Harper played with the Firehouse Five Plus Two, a Dixieland jazz band that included other Disney talents. He went on to work as an artist, set designer, and producer in Hollywood for many years. "Oriental Tattooing" refers to the fact that Harper wanted to open a tattoo parlor on Main Street, but Walt didn't think it would fit the wholesome image of Disneyland.

Laugh-O-gram
Films, Inc.
A Reel of Fun
W.E. Disney
Directing Animator

Walter Elias Disney founded Laugh-O-gram Studios in Kansas City, Missouri in 1921. It played a pivotal role, not only to the early years of animation, but to The Walt Disney Company itself. It was here that Walt, and his team of animators, produced the Laugh-O-gram animated series of modernized fairy tales, along with the first *Alice Comedy*. This Window is located in Mickey's Toontown, above the Library, and is the only Window in Disneyland that directly pays tribute to Walt. There are other Windows on the second story of Mickey's Toontown referencing many of Disney's cartoon characters, such as Toby Tortoise, Jiminy Cricket, and Scrooge McDuck.

Windows of Yesterland

Glasses Fitted
Nat Winecoff
Optometrist

Nat Winecoff had a Window located above the Silhouette Studio. Nat did a lot of work on the early planning of Disneyland, such as finding the perfect location for it. He was responsible for putting together the deal with Anaheim's city manager, Keith Murdoch, to help put Disneyland where Walt wanted it. Nat left Disney shortly after the Park opened, to start his own design firm, creating Disneyland-like amusement parks all over the United States, sometimes trying to steal some of Disney's talented artists away. It's likely that his Window was removed because of this.

Painting and Paperhanging
Larry Smith

Larry Smith had a Window that was located above Market House. He was the first Supervisor of the Disneyland Paint Shop.

Painless Dental Extractions

Buggies Wagons

Surreys Sleighs

Niagara
Magic Lantern
Slides

Fraternal Hall
Lodge Meetings

These Windows were for atmosphere only, and did not pay tribute to anyone.

Magic Kingdom

WALT DISNEY WORLD
RAILROAD OFFICE
KEEPING DREAMS ON TRACK
WALTER E. DISNEY
CHIEF ENGINEER

WALTER ELIAS DISNEY did not live long enough to see his dream of the Florida resort become a reality. Originally going to be called Disney World, Roy insisted that his brother's first name be used in the resort's name, to pay tribute to the man and his dreams. Walt's name appears on the Railroad station because he had a lifelong fascination with trains. Before Disneyland, Walt designed and built the Carolwood Pacific Railroad for his own backyard, a 1/8 scale version of a real train, so that he could spend his free time at home riding the rails.

BROGGIES BUGGIES
HAND MADE
WAGONS SURREYS SLEIGHS
ROGER BROGGIE
WHEELWRIGHT

ROGER E. BROGGIE is often considered to be the first Imagineer (aside from Walt) to work for WED Enterprises. Broggie joined the Studio in 1939 as a precision machinist. Once Walt learned Broggie was an avid railroad fan, he asked him to help design the layout of the Carolwood Pacific Railroad, which ran around Walt's Holmby Hills home. He also helped create the Lilly Belle, the miniature steam engine. In 1950, Broggie was promoted to Head of the Machine Shop, and created Academy Award-winning effects, such as the ones used in *20,000 Leagues Under The Sea*. Broggie went on to work on such attractions as the Disneyland Railroad, the Monorail, and the first life-size human Audio-Animatronic figure, Abraham Lincoln. Broggie retired in 1975.

OWEN POPE
HARNESS MAKER
FEED & GRAIN SUPPLIES LEATHER GOODS
"SADDLES A SPECIALTY"

OWEN POPE, along with his wife Dolly, was hired to help train the livestock at Disneyland. Because the training was fairly labor intensive, the Popes had to live as close as possible to the horses. So, Walt allowed Owen and Dolly to live at Disneyland, in the area behind Big Thunder Ranch. Their house is the only one that existed before Disneyland was built that still remains on property. The Popes moved to Florida in 1971 to supervise the building of Tri-Circle-D Ranch at Fort Wilderness. Owen stayed on to train the livestock at Walt Disney World until he retired in 1975.

PLAZA SCHOOL OF MUSIC
SHEET MUSIC
B. BAKER
BAND UNIFORMS
B. JACKMAN
MUSIC ROLLS
G. BRUNS

BUDDY BAKER composed the musical scores for many Disney films and television shows, such as *The Apple Dumpling Gang* and *The Fox and the Hound*. Before working for Disney, he was Musical Director for Bob Hope's radio show. He had a few big hits, and became a professor at the Los Angeles City College. In the 1950s, his friend George Bruns asked him to help compose music for *Davy Crockett and the River Pirates*, thus starting his career at Disney. Eventually, he became Music Director and Chief Composer for the Disney Parks, creating iconic pieces of music for the Haunted Mansion, If You Had Wings, and more.

BOB JACKMAN was the voice of Goofy for a few years during the 1950s. He was also Manager of Disney's Music Department. He specialized in writing cues: small snippets of music that were adapted from longer sections, which acted as lead-ins or lead-outs from scenes. He co-wrote the opening theme to *The Mickey Mouse Club*, and *Swisskapolka*, the catchy tune heard while climbing the Swiss Family Treehouse.

GEORGE BRUNS was hired by Walt Disney in 1953 as a musical arranger. Eventually, he became Disney's Musical Director, and kept that title until he retired in 1976. George is best known for co-writing the music for *The Ballad of Davy Crockett* and *Yo Ho (A Pirate's Life For Me)*. He sometimes also played with the Firehouse Five Plus Two.

Main Street Music Co.
Ron Logan
Conductor
"Leading the Band into a New Century"

Ron Logan was a professional musician since the ninth grade, and had performed trumpet for various television and movie scores. He was hired to play trumpet at Disneyland in the mid-1960s. Eventually, Ron worked his way up to Executive Vice President of Walt Disney Entertainment, where he was responsible for almost every aspect of live entertainment worldwide. Ron founded Disney Theatrical Productions, which has produced highly successful Broadway shows, starting with *Beauty and the Beast*. He retired from Disney in 2001.

Rainbow Paint Co.
Polychromatists
Lonnie R. Lindley
Worlds Largest Collection of Color Samples

Lonnie R. Lindley started his career at Disney by selling guidebooks at Disneyland. By 1963, he was working in the parts warehouse, assisting the maintenance department. Eventually, Lonnie met Walt while working on a painting project for the Plaza Inn. When a painter couldn't get it right, Walt asked Lonnie to do it. From there, Lonnie became known for having a keen eye for color. In 1970, he transferred to Florida, and was soon overseeing all paint operations at Walt Disney World. After serving as Superintendent for the Paint and Sign shops, he moved to ride and show engineering in 1998, where he worked until he retired in 2007.

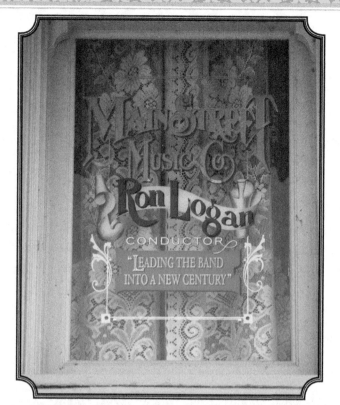

PROJECT DETECTIVE AGENCY
PRIVATE INVESTIGATIONS
WE NEVER SLEEP
ED BULLARD
INVESTIGATOR

ED BULLARD was a host at Disneyland and the Graveyard Supervisor at Walt Disney World when it opened. He was one of the first rangers to invade Normandy during World War II, and carried around the shiv from his gun in his boot during his career at Disney.

NEW ERA
BAND & CHOIR STUDIO
INSTRUCTION
ROBERT JANI
BANDMASTER

ROBERT F. "BOB" JANI started at Disneyland in 1955 as Director of Guest Relations at the age of 21. Though he left to form his own company in 1961, he returned in 1967 as Director of Entertainment. He was appointed Vice President of Entertainment in 1972 for both Disneyland and Walt Disney World, and helped produced some of the Park's most memorable parades, such as America on Parade and the much-loved Main Street Electrical Parade.

If It's New
It's the Latest
Talent Agents
Charles Corson
Casting Director

CHARLES CORSON was an executive in Disney's Entertainment Division. He later became Director of Entertainment for Disneyland and Walt Disney World.

Home Sweet Home
Interior Decorators
Emile Kuri
Proprietor

EMILE KURI joined Walt Disney Studios in 1952 as Chief Decorator for such films as *The Parent Trap*, *Mary Poppins*, and *20,000 Leagues Under The Sea*, for which he won an Academy Award. Emile's keen sense of style made him instrumental in the design of Disneyland, where he was the primary decorator for Walt's apartment above the Firehouse, the shops on Main Street, Club 33, and much more. He supervised the Disney exhibits at the 1964-65 New York World's Fair. Later, he was a design consultant for the Magic Kingdom. Emile retired in 1974.

RIDGWAY AND COMPANY
PUBLIC RELATIONS
CHARLES RIDGWAY
PRESS AGENT
"NO EVENT TOO SMALL"

CHARLES "CHARLIE" RIDGWAY was writing about Disney well before he worked for them. While working as a reporter, Charlie covered the building of the Park, and wrote some of the first articles to appear in major newspapers about Disneyland. He joined Disneyland's public relations office in 1963. He became Disneyland's Publicity Supervisor in 1966, and then Publicity Manager in 1969. By 1971, he was Director of Press and Publicity for Walt Disney World. During his time with Disney, he helped with over 200 major press events.

DOLLS BY MISS JOYCE
DOLLMAKER FOR THE WORLD
SHOPS IN
NEW YORK, CALIFORNIA, FLORIDA, JAPAN & PARIS
OWNER & FOUNDER
JOYCE CARLSON

JOYCE CARLSON started at Walt Disney Studios in 1944, delivering mail and office supplies. Over the course of several months, she put together an art portfolio, and presented it to her boss. She worked on such films as *Cinderella*, *Peter Pan*, and *Lady and the Tramp*. By 1960, she had moved over to work at WED Enterprises, to help create attractions for Disneyland and the 1964-1965 New York World's Fair. She designed many of the singing dolls for "it's a small world", hence her title of "Dollmaker for the World." Joyce continued in Imagineering until 2000, where she worked on other attractions, and also helped to bring "it's a small world" to Disney Parks all over the world.

RIDGWAY
and Company
PUBLIC
RELATIONS

Charles Ridgway   PRESS AGENT   "No event too small"

Dolls BY
Miss Joyce
Dollmaker for the World
Shops in
NEW YORK, CALIFORNIA, FLORIDA, JAPAN & PARIS

OWNER & FOUNDER JOYCE CARLSON

Little Gremlins Mechanical Toys
We build 'em – you run 'em
Toy Makers & Associates
Bob Booth   Roger Broggie, Jr.   John Franke
Neil Gallagher   John Gladish   Rudy Peña
Dave Schweninger   Dick Van Every   Jim Verity

Bob Booth worked in Walt Disney Studios' camera service department from 1957, before transferring to the machine shop in 1962. Bob was responsible for helping to set up MAPO (Manufacturing and Production Organization). MAPO developed many state-of-the-art technologies used in Disney Parks.

Roger Broggie Jr was the son of Roger E. Broggie. At the age of 18, he joined Disney as an apprentice in the machine shop managed by his dad. He became an Audio-Animatronics pioneer, and contributed to many iconic Disney attractions, such as Walt Disney's Enchanted Tiki Room, Country Bear Jamboree, and Pirates of the Caribbean.

John Franke worked in MAPO to help produce many iconic Audio-Animatronics, such as the birds for Walt Disney's Enchanted Tiki Room. He was a shop fabricator, which enabled him to build almost every kind of mechanism needed. John worked in an area of MAPO known as Pelican Alley, which got its name because so many animated birds were built there.

Neil Gallagher started work in Disney's machine shop in 1957, before building the flower boats, amongst other things, for Walt Disney's Enchanted Tiki Room. He helped to create the lifelike Lincoln figure for the 1964-1965 New York World's Fair. He stayed in New York to lend maintenance support for Disney's four shows in the Fair. After the Fair was over, he returned to lead the show and animation team at MAPO. When preparing to build Walt Disney World, Neil moved to Florida to become Director of Maintenance. He was moved in 1979 to help work on Tokyo Disneyland and then later Disneyland Paris.

Jack Gladish was an animation designer before moving over to WED Enterprises. He worked in MAPO on various projects, ranging from Great Moments with Mr. Lincoln for the 1964-1965 New York World's Fair to 20,000 Leagues Under The Sea: Submarine Voyage.

RUDY PEÑA was a mechanical engineer and department manager at MAPO. He was a union steward. He also worked in Pelican Alley.

DAVE SCHWENINGER was involved with the development of many of the Audio-Animatronics found in classic Disney attractions, such as the Haunted Mansion. He was also in charge of the animation shop at MAPO.

DICK VAN EVERY started as camera technician but, due to his reputation of being able to build anything, was moved over to MAPO to become a mechanical engineer. He also worked in Pelican Alley.

JIM VERITY was a third-generation *Disney* employee, since his father and grandfather had both worked at the Studios. In addition to working at MAPO, he became Manager of Show Quality Standards.

I Associates
Ken Klug Stan Maslak John Zovich

Ken Klug was a civil designer who started working at WED Enterprises in California before moving to work on Walt Disney World.

Stanley Maslak was a project engineer for WED Enterprises. He is most notable for his work on the Railroad stations at the Magic Kingdom.

John Zovich was Don Edgren's protégé, and was instrumental in the design and construction of the Magic Kingdom and Epcot. He was Vice President of Engineering for Epcot during its construction.

I Super Structures Inc.
Engineers and Associates
Don Edgren John Wise
Partners

Don Edgren worked at Disneyland in its very early stages. As one of the engineers for Wheeler & Gray, the engineering firm in charge of the structural design of the Park, Don became Chief Engineer onsite in 1954. He worked for Wheeler & Gray until being hired by WED Enterprises in 1961, where he went on to work on attractions for the 1964-1965 New York World's Fair and Disneyland. He was Head of Field Engineering for Walt Disney World during its construction, and Director of Engineering for Tokyo Disneyland.

John Wise was originally employed by Wheeler & Gray before working in several engineering positions for WED Enterprises and the Buena Vista Construction Company. Eventually, he became Chief Engineer of Disneyland. In 1974, he was the first President of the Community Transportation Division of Walt Disney Productions.

I ASSOCIATES
MORRIE HOUSER
LOU JENNINGS
JOHN JOYCE

MORRIE HOUSER became an Imagineer in 1954. He worked on many Disney attractions, though his specialties were the Railroads at both Disneyland and Walt Disney World. He was working on his own version of Walt's 1/8 scale Lilly Belle from the Carolwood Pacific Railroad, but passed away before its completion.

LOU JENNINGS was an Imagineer at WED Enterprises.

JOHN JOYCE was an Imagineer at WED Enterprises.

"OSH" POPHAM
PROPRIETOR

"OSH" POPHAM is a fictional character played by Burl Ives in the 1963 Disney film *Summer Magic*. "Osh" was a shopkeeper, amongst other things, in Beulah, Maine who helped Hayley Mills' family find a new home.

I

Associates

MORRIE HOUSER
LOU JENNINGS
JOHN JOYCE

COMBO PACK

"OSH" POPHAM
PROPRIETOR

THE HUMAN DYNAMO
CALCULATING MACHINE CO.
MICHAEL BAGNALL
OFFICE MGR.
DAVID SNYDER
PROGRAM SUPERVISOR

MICHAEL BAGNALL was the son of George Bagnall, a former member of the Board of Directors. Michael started in a low-level position in the finance department, but quickly climbed the ranks to become Chief Financial Officer for The Walt Disney Company.

DAVID SNYDER was Head of DACS (Digital Animation Control System), which is the computer system used to control all the attractions at Walt Disney World.

WALSH'S CHIMNEY SWEEP & PEST CONTROL CO.
PROFESSOR BILL WALSH
THE BUG LOVER
CINCINNATI, OHIO
BURBANK CALIF.

BILL WALSH was one of Disney's top writers and movie producers. He started out in Disney's publicity department, where he wrote the Mickey Mouse comic strips. Walt enjoyed his work so much, he asked him to write for some of his television shows, such as *The Mickey Mouse Club* and *Davy Crockett*. Soon, he was writing feature films, such as *The Shaggy Dog*, *The Absent-Minded Professor*, *The Love Bug*, and *Mary Poppins*. His Window refers to *Mary Poppins* ("Chimney Sweep"), *The Love Bug* ("The Bug Lover"), and *The Absent-Minded Professor* (the second "s" in "Professor" is supposed to look like it was added later, like someone absentmindedly forgot it).

PETERSON TRAVEL AGENCY
RESERVATIONS BY CABLE
ANYWHERE IN THE WORLD
EXCLUSIVE REPRESENTATIVES OF THE TITANIC
PASSAGES BOOKED BY SEA & RAIL
JACK LINDQUIST
PURSER

JACK LINDQUIST was hired by Walt in 1955 as the first Advertising Manager of Disneyland. He is known for helping create some of the most memorable Disney traditions, such as the Magic Kingdom Club, Disney Dollars, the Disneyland Ambassador Program, Grad Nite, and the "E" tickets. He was promoted to Director of Marketing in 1965. He helped to set up the marketing department at Walt Disney World, and was named Vice President of Marketing for both resorts in 1972. He was given the title of President of Disneyland in 1990.

ROBINSON'S REPAIRS
RESTORATIONS AND RENOVATIONS
NO JOB TOO LARGE OR...TOO SMALL
CECIL ROBINSON
PROPRIETOR

CECIL ROBINSON worked for 10 years in the finance department before becoming Vice President of Facility Services for The Walt Disney Company.

The Big Wheel Co.
One of a Kind
Horseless Carriages   Unicycles
Dave Gengenbach   Bob Gurr
George McGinnis   Bill Watkins

Dave Gengenbach started working for WED Enterprises in 1966 as a project manager and engineer. Eventually, he became Vice President of WED. He oversaw the design and installation of many of the Magic Kingdom's most popular attractions, including 20,000 Leagues Under The Sea: Submarine Voyage and Space Mountain. He also designed the Mark III and Mark IV Monorails.

Bob Gurr was hired out of art school to consult on the design of the Autopia cars. What followed was a career that spanned almost four decades. He has developed over 100 designs for all sorts of vehicles, from the Matterhorn Bobsleds, the Monorail, to the vehicles on Main Street, and more. If it is on wheels at Disneyland, chances are that Bob designed it. Though he had no formal training in engineering, Bob took it upon himself to learn, and his skills are unsurpassed.

George McGinnis joined WED Enterprises in 1966 after impressing Walt Disney with a working model of a high-speed train which had been his senior project for college. His first task for WED was designing transportation models for the Progress City display once seen at the end of Carousel of Progress. George went on to have a hand in creating some of Walt Disney World's most memorable attractions, such as the WEDWay PeopleMover and Horizons. He also designed the Mark VI Monorail.

Bill Watkins worked for Lockheed Aircraft Corporation before joining WED Enterprises as a project engineer. He contributed to the design of many of the ride vehicles at both Disneyland and Walt Disney World. He is considered one of the forefathers of the modern roller coaster.

OPEN SINCE '71
MAGIC KINGDOM
CASTING AGENCY
"IT TAKES PEOPLE TO MAKE THE DREAM A REALITY"
WALTER ELIAS DISNEY
FOUNDER & DIRECTOR EMERITUS

WALTER ELIAS DISNEY is the name on this Window, although it is actually a tribute to all Walt Disney World Cast Members, past and present.

YUCATAN ENGINE WORKS
BOILER & ENGINE SPECIALISTS
HIGHEST GRADE STEAM POWER
EARL VILMER
CONSULTANT

EARL VILMER was a transportation superintendent at Walt Disney World. His Window refers to the fact that he traveled to Yucatan, Mexico to purchase four steam engines from United Railways to be used at Magic Kingdom. Once they were brought back to Tampa, Earl was in charge of their restoration before they went on to live at Walt Disney World.

Dr. Card Walker
Licensed Practitioner of Psychiatry
and
Justice of the Peace
We Never Close
Except for Golf

E. Cardon "Card" Walker started working for The Walt Disney Company in 1938, in the mailroom, and rose through the ranks fairly quickly. He was promoted to Vice President of Advertising and Sales in 1956, then Vice President of Marketing in 1965, Executive Vice President of Operations in 1967, and Chief Operating Officer in 1968. In 1976, he became the first Chief Executive to not be a member of the Disney family, and in 1980, he was appointed Chairman of the Board. Card would often be the intermediary between Walt and Roy, hence the "Justice of the Peace" portion of his Window. He also loved golf, which accounts for the last line.

Main Street
Youth Athletic League
"Preparing Youngsters for the Game of Life"
Al Weiss
Head Coach

Al Weiss started at Walt Disney World in 1972 as a financial analyst. He worked hard over the years, and became President of Walt Disney World in 1994. He served in that role until 2005, when he became President of Worldwide Operations for Disney Parks and Resorts.

MAIN STR.
WATER WORKS
LET US SOLVE YOUR PLUMBING PROBLEMS
CONTROL SYSTEMS
MAINTENANCE
TED CROWELL
CHIEF ENGINEER
ARNOLD LINDBERG
FOREIGN REP.

EDWARD B. "TED" CROWELL started as an engineer at Disneyland in 1958, helping to study ride capacities, and to forecast attendance of the Park. He became Director of Maintenance in 1966. He was one of the 25 people sent to Florida by Walt Disney to secretly research the area for what would become Walt Disney World. By 1970, he was Director of Maintenance for both Disneyland and Walt Disney World, and then finally became Vice President of Facilities for Walt Disney World.

ARNOLD LINDBERG immigrated to the United States in 1951, and became a mechanic for Disneyland in the machine shop. His first assignment was to make a timing device for the time-lapse camera that recorded the construction of Disneyland. After that, he would oversee the restoration of two of the trains that would become part of the Disneyland Railroad. By the time Walt Disney World was being built, he had become the technical head of all workshops. He also contributed to the construction of both Disneyland Paris and Tokyo Disneyland. He is listed as a "Foreign Rep." because he was born in Sweden.

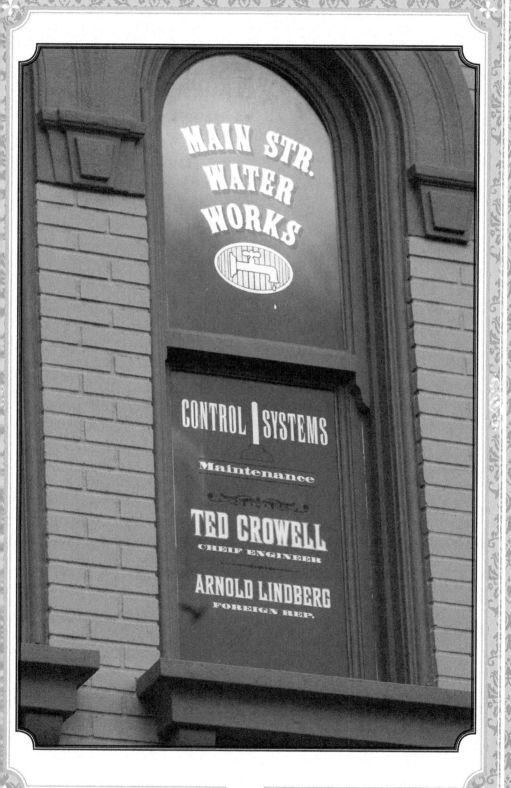

Big Top
Theatrical Productions
Famous Since '55
Shows for World's Fairs and International Expositions
Claude Coats   Marc Davis
John De Cuir   Bill Justice

Claude Coats was a background artist for the animation department. He moved to WED Enterprises in 1955, and soon became a show designer. He was involved in the development of the Haunted Mansion, Pirates of the Caribbean, the Submarine Voyage, and other iconic attractions. He went on to design for almost all the Disney Parks in the world.

Marc Davis was one of Walt's famous "Nine Old Men." He was responsible for developing such characters as Cinderella and Tinker Bell. In 1961, Walt asked Davis to move to WED Enterprises, to help develop story concepts, character designs, and gags for some of the Disneyland attractions. His sketches for the Haunted Mansion, Pirates of the Caribbean, and the Jungle Cruise are some of the most well-known Disney concept art. Though he retired in 1978, he continued to contribute designs for Epcot and Tokyo Disneyland.

John De Cuir Jr. worked as a designer on many of Walt Disney World's attractions, such as The Hall of Presidents and Space Mountain. He also worked on the design of the Polynesian and the Contemporary Resorts. He left Disney for a while, but returned in 1974 to work on the master plan for Epcot.

Bill Justice joined The Walt Disney Company as an animator in 1937, and joined WED Enterprises in 1965 at the behest of Walt. He programmed many of the Audio-Animatronic figures for Mission to Mars, Pirates of the Caribbean, Great Moments with Mr. Lincoln, and more. He was also involved in creating the spectacular costumes used in many of the Disneyland parades, including the very first Disneyland Christmas parade and the Main Street Electrical Parade.

CHINESE RESTAURANT
FINE FOOD
IMPORTED TEA
JIM ARMSTRONG
VEGETABLE BUYER

JIM ARMSTRONG worked as Executive Chef for many Florida restaurants before he became Vice President of Resorts and Foods Administration at Walt Disney World.

MERCHANTS HOTEL
FIRST CLASS IN PARTICULARS
STEAM HEAT THROUGHOUT
JOHN CURRY   OWNER REPRESENTATIVE
HOWARD ROLAND   FURNISHINGS
STAN GARVES   ENGINEERING

JOHN CURRY met Walt Disney in Yosemite National Park, while Walt was in the planning phases for the proposed Mineral King Ski Resort. Because John and his family had a lot of experience in hospitality, Walt hired him as Disneyland's first hotel employee in 1966. John went on to help conceive and operate the Polynesian and the Contemporary Resorts.

HOWARD ROLAND originally worked for US Steel, the company that built some of Walt Disney World's original resorts, but left to become Disney's Vice President of Construction Contract Administration and Purchasing.

STAN GRAVES worked with WED Enterprises on the engineering of some of the original Walt Disney World hotels. His name is spelled incorrectly on the Window.

THE CAMELOT CORP.
ROAD SHOW INSTALLATIONS
TONY BAXTER   DAVE BURKHART
ED JOHNSON   GARY YOUNGER

TONY BAXTER started his career at Disney in 1965, serving ice cream at Carnation Plaza Gardens. He went on to work in the Parks in various roles until he joined Imagineering in 1970. He was made Senior Vice President of Imagineering, and held that title until he retired in 2013.

DAVE BURKHART started as a model maker with Disney in 1967. He went on to become a show designer and art producer for many attractions, such as 20,000 Leagues Under The Sea: Submarine Voyage, and the Haunted Mansion. He was named Superintendent of Decoration at Disneyland, before moving on to Tokyo Disneyland, where he was promoted to Vice President of Imagineering's International Show Quality Standards.

ED JOHNSON worked in the model shop at WED Enterprises, and became a show designer for some of Walt Disney World's attractions.

GARY YOUNGER worked at WED Enterprises as a production director, a system developer, and Director of MAPO.

THE RALPH KENT COLLECTION
FINE ARTS AND COLLECTIBLES
ANAHEIM   LAKE BUENA VISTA   TOKYO

RALPH KENT started as an artist in Disney's marketing department. He helped to create the promotional materials for the Jungle Cruise, Walt Disney's Enchanted Tiki Room, and more. He was responsible for designing the first limited-edition Mickey Mouse watch. Ralph also designed souvenirs, such as license plates and bumper stickers, for Walt Disney World's opening. Later, he was appointed Director of Walt Disney Imagineering East and then as a trainer for the Disney Design Group.

WALTER E. DISNEY
GRADUATE SCHOOL OF DESIGN & MASTER PLANNING
HEAD MASTER RICHARD IRVINE
DEAN OF DESIGN JOHN HENCH
INSTRUCTORS
HOWARD BRUMMITT MARVIN DAVIS FRED HOPE
VIC GREENE BILL MARTIN CHUCK MYALL

RICHARD F. "DICK" IRVINE was hired by Walt Disney in 1952 to act as liaison between Walt Disney Productions and the architectural firm that was being considered to build Disneyland. During the early 1960s, he supervised the attractions that Disney was building for the 1964-65 New York World's Fair. In 1967, Irvine was appointed Vice President and Chief Operations Officer of WED Enterprises. He helped develop the master plan for Walt Disney World, and continued to oversee Disney attractions until retiring in 1973.

JOHN HENCH began his career at Disney in 1939 as a sketch artist on *Fantasia*. He worked in many areas of the Studios before moving to WED Enterprises in 1954. From there, he helped design attractions for the Park and for the 1964-1965 New York World's Fair. He continued working in Imagineering up until his death in 2004, and was the longest-serving Disney employee, having been with the Company for 65 years. He was a true renaissance man, having worked as an artist, storyteller, and color designer.

HOWARD BRUMMITT was a designer at WED Enterprises, and was Lead Designer for Frontierland at the Magic Kingdom.

MARVIN DAVIS was recruited by Richard Irvine in 1953 to help with the design of Disneyland. After the Park opened in 1955, Davis became an art director for some of Disney's films and television shows. He returned to WED Enterprises in 1965 as a project designer for Walt Disney World. He helped to design some of its original hotels, such as the Polynesian Resort and the Contemporary. Davis married Walt's niece, Marjorie Sewell.

FRED HOPE SR. worked for WED Enterprises and helped with architectural projects for Disneyland, Walt Disney World, and Tokyo Disneyland.

VIC GREENE was an art director at WED Enterprises. He contributed designs to a number of attractions, including the Haunted Mansion.

WILSON "BILL" MARTIN joined WED Enterprises in 1953 as an art director and project designer for Disneyland attractions. He also created the master layout for the Magic Kingdom, including the Utilidor system, and helped with the design of Cinderella Castle. Before he retired in 1977, he was the architectural designer for the Italy and Mexico pavilions at Epcot.

CHUCK MYALL worked as an art director and designer for WED Enterprises. He worked on many attractions, including Sleeping Beauty Castle and Pirates of the Caribbean. He was one of the master planners for Walt Disney World.

FPC Academy
Featuring the Culinary Arts
Larry Slocum
Headmaster
Specializing In The "86" Steps to Gastronomical Expertise

Larry Slocum was Director of Food Operations at the Magic Kingdom when it opened, and went on to become Vice President of Food Operations for Walt Disney World.

Sully's Safaris & Guide Service
Chief Guide
Bill Sullivan

William "Sully" Sullivan was working for Northrop Aircraft Corporation when he watched the televised opening of Disneyland. By the next week, he had quit his job and was working as a ticket taker for the Jungle Cruise. Bill worked his way up to Operations Supervisor for the Park, and then Assistant Manager for Disney's attractions at the 1964-1965 New York World's Fair. In 1971, he moved to Florida to become Director of the Project Installation and Coordination Office for Walt Disney World. Later, he became Director of Epcot Operations, and finally was named Vice President of the Magic Kingdom in 1987.

COMMUNITY SERVICE RECRUITMENT CENTER
FOUNDER
BOB MATHEISON
QUALITY, INTEGRITY & DEDICATION

BOB MATHEISON started his career at Disney in 1960 as a sound coordinator at Disneyland, where he was responsible for everything that Guests could hear. Soon after, he became Manager of Guest Relations, and then Operations Manager for all of Disney's attractions at the 1964-1965 New York World's Fair. After the Fair, Bob headed up the research and development team for Walt Disney World. In 1969, he became Director of Operations at Disneyland, and then moved to Florida to become Director of Operations at Walt Disney World. By 1972, Bob had been promoted to Vice President of Operations, and in 1982 to Vice President of the Magic Kingdom and Epcot. In 1985, he became Executive Vice President of Walt Disney World.

Lazy M
Cattle Company of Wyoming
Ron & Diane Miller & Partners
Christopher Joanna Tamara Jennifer
Walter Ronald Jr. Patrick

Ronald William Miller was married to Diane Disney, Walt's daughter. He worked as liaison between WED Enterprises and Disneyland for a few years, before being drafted into the US Army. When he was discharged, he played as tight end for the Los Angeles Rams for a season before Walt got him a job as Second Assistant Director on *Old Yeller*. He soon started producing various Disney films, and even directed Walt a few times on television. Later, he became President of Walt Disney Productions in 1980, and then CEO in 1983.

Diane Disney Miller was the eldest daughter of Walt and Lillian Disney. She married Ron Miller in May 1954, and they had their first child, Christopher, in December 1954. Diane and Ron opened Silverado Vineyards Winery in 1981. Diane was always a champion of her father, and helped to plan the Walt Disney Concert Hall in Los Angeles, and organized the development of The Walt Disney Family Museum in San Francisco.

Christopher D. Miller is the oldest son of Ron Miller and Diane Disney Miller, and Walt's first grandchild. Miller worked as an assistant director on several films, such as *The Black Hole* and *Herbie Goes Bananas*.

Joanna Miller is the daughter of Ron and Diane, and was born in 1956.

Tamara Scheer is the daughter of Ron and Diane, and was born in 1957.

Jennifer Miller-Goff is the daughter of Ron and Diane, and was born in 1960.

Walter Miller is the son of Ron and Diane, and was born in 1961.

Ronald Miller Jr. is the son of Ron and Diane, and was born in 1963.

Patrick Miller is the son of Ron and Diane, and was born in 1967.

UB IWERKS met Walt Disney in 1919 in Kansas City, and the two went into business together soon after. Ub was responsible for many of Disney's earliest cartoons. When Walt began his Laugh-O-gram series in 1922, Ub was Chief Animator. He followed Walt to Los Angeles to work on the *Alice Comedies* and the Oswald the Lucky Rabbit cartoons. Ub was the primary designer of Mickey Mouse for Walt. Throughout the years, Ub worked on and off for The Walt Disney Company, helping them to create the process that combined animation and live action, and the xerographic process for cel animation. He also worked for WED Enterprises for a while, contributing to "it's a small world", The Hall of Presidents, and more.

DON IWERKS was the son of Ub Iwerks. He helped to create Circle-Vision 360, Star Tours, and many other film projects for the Disney Parks.

ROBERT "BUD" WASHO was a senior designer for WED Enterprises. He also headed the staff shop, which created all of the concrete and plastic work for Disneyland, from 1955 until 1967. Later in his career, he was Manager of Architectural Ornamentation for Epcot's World Showcase.

BILL WASHO was Bud's brother, and helped him design many of the Magic Kingdom's facades.

THE ORIGINAL DICK NUNIS GYM
NIGHT MANAGER
RON MILLER
24 HR. SERVICE

RONALD WILLIAM MILLER was married to Diane Disney, Walt's daughter. He became President of Walt Disney Productions in 1980, and then CEO in 1983.

TURKISH BATHS
SUPERVISOR
DICK NUNIS

RICHARD "DICK" NUNIS was promoted to Executive Vice President of Walt Disney World and Disneyland in 1971, and served as member of the Board of Directors from 1981 to 1999.

MASSAGE PARLOR
MASSEUR
O. FERRANTE

ORLANDO FERRANTE was a 40-year veteran of The Walt Disney Company, having overseen the engineering, design production, and installation of Disney Parks all around the world. He joined the Company in 1962, formed PICO (Project Installation Coordinating Office), and retired with the title of Vice President of Engineering, Design and Production.

Roy E. Disney
Specializing in the Gentlemanly Sport of
Racing at Sea
Aboard the Ketch
Peregrina
Sail Maker
Sailing Lessons
Patty Disney
First Mate and Gourmet Cook
Roy Patrick   Abigail   Susan   Timothy

Roy Edward Disney was the son of Roy O. Disney, and Walt Disney's nephew. He began his career at Disney in 1951 as an assistant director and producer for the *True-Life Adventure* series. He was elected to the Board of Directors in 1967. Throughout the years, he was the spearhead of two separate "Save Disney" campaigns: the first ousted Ron Miller, and the second resulted in Michael Eisner's retirement. He is also notable for serving as a consultant for the Company for many years and being Director Emeritus for the Board of Directors. In his personal life, he was an avid sailor, and held many sailing speed records.

Patricia Ann "Patty" Dailey Disney was married to Roy E. Disney from 1955 until 2007.

Roy Patrick Disney was the son of Roy and Patty.

Abigail Disney was the daughter of Roy and Patty and was born in 1960. She is known for her documentaries on social issues.

Susan Disney was the daughter of Roy and Patty.

Timothy Disney was the son of Roy and Patty.

Evans & Assoc.
Tree Surgeons
We grow 'em   You show 'em
Morgan Evans   D.T.S.
Tony Virginia   A.T.S.

Morgan "Bill" Evans was Director of Landscape Design for WED Enterprises.

Tony Virginia was Director of Horticulture for Walt Disney World.

M.T. Lott
Real Estate   Investments   Subsidiaries
A Friend in Deeds Is a Friend Indeed
Donn Tatum   President
Tomahawk Properties   Latin American Development
Ayefour Corporation   Bay Lake Properties
Reedy Creek Ranch Lands   Compass East Corporation

Donn Tatum joined Disney in 1956 as a production business manager after spending years working in radio and television. He was Roy O. Disney's right-hand man. After Roy O. Disney passed away in 1971, Donn became Chief Executive Officer and Chairman of the Board, making him the first non-Disney to head the Company. He stayed on as CEO until 1976, and as Chairman until 1980. Donn served as a director of The Walt Disney Company until 1992, when he was named Director Emeritus. He played a major role in the creation of the Magic Kingdom, Epcot, and Tokyo Disneyland. The businesses mentioned on the Window were shell companies that The Walt Disney Company created in order to hide the fact that they were buying land to build Walt Disney World. In addition, these names have a hidden meaning. For example, "M.T. Lott" is a play on words for "Empty Lot", "Ayefour Corporation" is a play on words for "I-4", the highway closest to Walt Disney World, and "Bay Lake Properties" is the name of a lake near the Magic Kingdom.

EVANS LANDSCAPE
TREE SURGEONS

We grow'em

You show'em

MORGAN EVANS
DES
TONY VIRGINIA
ATS

M'LOTT

REAL ESTATE
INVESTMENTS

... IS A FRIEND INDEED

DONN TATUM
PRESIDENT

M'LOTT

REAL ESTATE
INVESTMENTS

... WE HAVE PROPERTIES
LATIN AMERICAN
DEVELOPMENT
AYEFOUR CORPORATION
BAY LAKE PROPERTIES
REEDY CREEK RANCH LANDS
COMPASS EAST CORPORATION

Seven Summits Expeditions
Frank G. Wells President
"For those who want to do it all"

Frank G. Wells was The Walt Disney Company's President and Chief Operating Officer, beginning in 1984. He passed away in a helicopter crash in 1994. "Seven Summits Expeditions" honors his goal to scale the seven continents' tallest peaks. This Window is the highest in the Park, located on the third story, to further that connection.

The Double Check Co.
"A Penny Saved Is A Penny Earned"
B. Franklin Auditors and Bookkeepers
Larry Tryon Mike Bagnall Carl Bongirno
Jim McManus Warren Robertson

Benjamin Franklin was one of the Founding Fathers of the United States. He famously once said "A Penny Saved Is A Penny Earned."

Larry Tryon was Treasurer of Walt Disney Productions.

Michael Bagnall was the son of George Bagnall, a former member of the Board of Directors. Michael started in a low-level position in the finance department, but quickly climbed the ranks to become Chief Financial Officer for The Walt Disney Company.

Carl Bongirno worked as Treasurer of WED Enterprises for 4 years. He became Vice President of Finance, and Treasurer, for Walt Disney World from 1972 until 1979. He was also President of WED for a few years.

Jim McManus worked in the finance department at WED Enterprises, and was Director of Finance for Walt Disney World.

Warren Robertson worked in the finance department at WED Enterprises.

FENSE BROS.
ATTORNEYS-AT-LAW
D. FENSE   O. FENSE
PARTNERS   LEGAL ASSOCIATES
NEAL McCLURE   DICK MORROW   SPENCE OLIN
JIM ROSS   PHIL SMITH

D. FENSE is not a real person, but a play on words for "defense."

O. FENSE is not a real person, but a play on words for "offense."

NEAL McCLURE was Lead Counsel in the Disneyland legal department, and was considered one of "Roy's Boys," people who Roy O. Disney could trust with WED Enterprises' legal matters.

RICHARD T. "DICK" MORROW served as General Counsel for Walt Disney Productions and was on the Board of Directors from 1971 to 1984.

SPENCER OLIN was one of the Studio's attorneys, who specialized in contract law.

JIM ROSS was one of the Studio's attorneys.

PHIL SMITH was hired as legal counsel when the final few land plots that became Walt Disney World were being purchased. He was the first permanent Cast Member, and lived on the property as its only resident during construction. When Walt Disney World opened in 1971, Phil was in charge of its day-to-day legal issues. In 1973, he became Vice President of the Legal Department.

DYER PREDICTION & PRESTIDIGITADICATION
A FLORIDA INSTITUTION SINCE '67
BONAR DYER
PRESIDENT

BONAR DYER was Vice President of Industrial Relations for Walt Disney Productions.

THE BACK LOT
PROPS & SCENIC BACKDROPS
FRANK MILLINGTON
CHUCK FOWLER
HANK DAINS
MARSHALL SMELSER

FRANK MILLINGTON worked in the decoration department, which created most of the props and backdrops that makes Walt Disney World feel like a lived-in place.

CHARLES E. "CHUCK" FOWLER JR. worked in the decoration department and the maintenance department for Walt Disney World.

HANK DAINS was an opening day Cast Member at Disneyland, where he worked in the furnishings department. When he moved to Walt Disney World, he was made Manager of the Decoration Department.

MARSHALL SMELSER worked in the decoration department at Walt Disney World.

PROPS
& SCENIC
BACKDROPS

FRANK MILLINGTON
CHUCK FOWLER
HANK DAINS
MARSHALL SMELSER

WINDERMERE FRATERNAL HALL
CHARTER MEMBERS
BOB ALLEN   PETE CRIMMINGS   DICK EVANS
BILL HOELSCHER   BOB MATHEISON   BILL SULLIVAN

ROBERT "BOB" ALLEN started his career at Disney working on Casey Jr. Circus Train in Disneyland in 1955. Eventually, he became Manager of The Golden Horseshoe Saloon, and then Manager of Guest Relations. In 1964, he moved to Colorado to manage Disney's Celebrity Sports Center, a family recreation spot. He returned to Disneyland in 1968 as Staff Assistant to the Vice President of the Park, and as Director of General Services. Just before Walt Disney World opened, he moved to Florida to become Director of their General Services, and was later named Vice President of Resorts. He was promoted to Vice President of Walt Disney World in 1977, where he served until passing away in 1987.

PETE CRIMMINGS was an executive for Walt Disney World Operations.

DICK EVANS was an executive for Walt Disney World Operations.

BILL HOELSCHER started his career at Disney on the Jungle Cruise. He later became the recruiter for the Disney attractions at the 1964-1965 New York World's Fair. He was in charge of cast activities at Walt Disney World.

BOB MATHEISON started his career at Disney in 1960 as a sound coordinator at Disneyland. In 1969, he became Director of Operations at Disneyland, and then moved to Florida to become Director of Operations at Walt Disney World. By 1972, Bob had been promoted to Vice President of Operations, and in 1982 to Vice President of the Magic Kingdom and Epcot. In 1985, he became Executive Vice President of Walt Disney World.

WILLIAM "SULLY" SULLIVAN was working for Northrop Aircraft Corporation when he watched the televised opening of Disneyland. By the next week, he had quit his job and was working as a ticket taker for the Jungle Cruise. Bill worked his way up to Operations Supervisor for the Park, and then Assistant Manager for Disney's attractions at the 1964-1965 New York World's Fair. In 1971, he moved to Florida to become Director of the Project Installation and Coordination Office for Walt Disney World. Later, he became Director of Epcot Operations, and finally was named Vice President of the Magic Kingdom in 1987.

OLSEN'S IMPORTS
SOUVENIRS
NOVELTIES
"WORLD'S LARGEST COLLECTION OF KEYCHAINS"
JACK OLSEN
THE MERCHANT PRINCE

JACK OLSEN started as a background artist for Walt Disney Studios in 1955. Soon, he became Manager of the Stores at Disneyland, due to his background in operating art supply stores and galleries in Los Angeles. In 1960, he was moved to the merchandising department as Manager of Product and Project Design and Development. By 1970, he was Vice President of Merchandising. His Window alludes to the fact that he kept the stores stocked with all the souvenirs and novelties that Guests would want to bring home.

VOICE & SINGING
PRIVATE LESSONS
MUSIC & DANCE LESSONS
BALLET TAP & WALTZ

This Window is for atmosphere only, and does not pay tribute to anyone. However, every so often you can hear a tap lesson coming from the Window.

SAYERS & COMPANY
COLLEGE OF BUSINESS
JACK SAYERS
NATIONAL REP.

JACK SAYERS was Chairman of Disneyland's Park Operating Committee from 1956 to 1959. In 1968, he became Vice President of Lessee Relations for Disneyland and Walt Disney World.

SATISFIED GRADUATES
FROM COAST TO COAST
PETE CLARK
WESTERN MGR.

PETE CLARK was Director of Lessee Relations for Disneyland, hence the "Western Mgr." under his name.

REFERENCES ON REQUEST
NORM FAGRELL
EASTERN MGR.

NORM FAGRELL was Director of Lessee Relations for Walt Disney World, hence the "Eastern Mgr." under his name.

GENERAL CONTRACTOR
BUD DARE
WE "DARE" YOU TO FIND A BETTER DEAL
REEDY CREEK
BAY LAKE
LAKE BUENA VISTA

BUD DARE was Vice President of Operations Management at Walt Disney World, and would later become Vice President of Facilities and Development.

REFERENCES
ON REQUEST

NORM FAGRELL
EASTERN MGR.

GENERAL
CONTRACTOR
BUD DARE

We Dare You to
Find a Better Deal

Reedy Creek - Bay Lake
Lake Buena Vista

CENTER STREET
ACADEMY OF FINE ART
PAINTING & SCULPTURE
COLLIN CAMPBELL   HERBERT RYMAN   BLAINE GIBSON
MARY BLAIR   DOROTHEA REDMOND

COLLIN CAMPBELL started working at Disney in 1943, as a messenger. He left in 1944 when he was drafted into the US Navy, but returned for a short stint in 1946 in the traffic department. After putting himself through art school, he became an inbetweener in 1952, where he worked on such films as *Lady and the Tramp* and *Sleeping Beauty*. He designed many of the sets for *The Mickey Mouse Club* and the *Disneyland* television show. Campbell moved to WED Enterprises to help with Walt Disney's Enchanted Tiki Room, and to contribute to the 1964-1965 New York World's Fair projects. He helped design Club 33, and helped develop Pirates of the Caribbean. His illustrations for *The Story and Song from the Haunted Mansion* album book are his best known work. He helped develop much of the design and feel of the Magic Kingdom. He contributed designs for Epcot, Disney's Hollywood Studios, and Disneyland Paris.

HERBERT "HERB" RYMAN spent a weekend holed up with Walt in September 1953, which produced the very first defining image of Disneyland. He went on to create iconic concept sketches of the Magic Kingdom, Epcot, and Tokyo Disneyland, even after he officially retired in 1971.

BLAINE GIBSON joined Walt Disney Studios in 1939 as an animator. Walt saw some of his sculptures, and recruited him to work for WED Enterprises. Blaine became Head of the Sculpture Studio at WED, and helped create some of the memorable figures you now see at Disney Parks worldwide.

MARY ROBINSON BLAIR joined Disney in 1940 to work in animation. She was the only female animator to go on the South American trip that resulted in *Saludos Amigos* and *The Three Caballeros*, where she is credited as an art supervisor. She went on to create concept art and color styling for *Cinderella*, *Peter Pan*, *Alice in Wonderland*, and more. She left Disney after *Peter Pan* to work freelance, illustrating several Little Golden Books. She returned to Disney, at Walt's request, to work on "it's a small world" for the 1964-1965 New York World's Fair, and also when it moved to Disneyland. She designed the 90-foot mural at the Contemporary, which features the infamous Five Legged Goat.

DOROTHEA HOLT REDMOND was very successful in the 1940s and 1950s for her collaborations with Alfred Hitchcock, where her illustrations helped set the tone and mood for seven of his films. She began working at WED Enterprises in 1966, where she helped design New Orleans Square. She went on to design much of Fantasyland and Main Street at the Magic Kingdom.

FAMILY MORTGAGE TRUST
MUNICIPAL STOCKS AND BONDS
LOANS AND DEDENTURES
INTEREST LOW   TERMS FAVORABLE   NO DELAY
NOLAN BROWNING, COUNSELOR

NOLAN BROWNING was a financial expert and an attorney. Nolan is credited with introducing Roy O. Disney to debenture bonds. These bonds helped Roy raise the money to build Walt Disney World without having to merge with another company.

PSEUDONYM
REAL ESTATE DEVELOPMENT COMPANY
ROY DAVIS   PRESIDENT
BOB PRICE   VICE-PRESIDENT
BOB FOSTER   TRAVELING REPRESENTATIVE

ROY OLIVER DISNEY was Walt Disney's older brother, partner, and co-founder of The Walt Disney Company. While Walt took the spotlight and came up with the ideas, Roy was the behind-the-scenes man who did everything he could to make sure his brother's dreams, from the animated films to the theme parks, were financially possible. He became the unofficial CEO in 1929, but was not officially given the title until 1968. He shared the title of Chairman of the Board with Walt. Roy postponed his retirement after Walt's death to oversee the construction of the Florida Project. He renamed the project from Disney World to Walt Disney World to pay tribute to his brother. He used the name Roy Davis to secretly buy the land that would become Walt Disney World.

ROBERT "BOB" PRICE FOSTER was legal counsel for Disneyland, and in 1964 was made responsible for finding the land that would eventually become Walt Disney World. Foster also played a significant role in the development and implementation of the legislative package for Walt Disney World. When he was secretly buying the land for Walt Disney World, he used the name Bob Price.

Elias Disney
Contractor
Est. 1895

Elias Disney was the father of Walt and Roy Disney. Though born in Canada, he moved his family to wherever he could find carpentry work. He was a hard worker, and Walt attributed his hardworking attitude as coming from his father.

Golden State
Graphic Arts Studio
Latest Artistic Principles Employed
Ken Chapman   Sam McKim   Paul Hartley
Elmer Plummer   Ernie Prinzhorn

Ken Chapman was a design specialist at WED Enterprises. He was responsible for creating iconic attraction posters, such as for Carousel of Progress, PeopleMover, and the Haunted Mansion.

Sam McKim was a former child actor who started to work for WED Enterprises in 1954. He is probably best known for his Disneyland souvenir maps, which were sold between 1958 and 1964.

Paul Hartley originally worked in Disney's animation department, but went on to be a design specialist for WED Enterprises. He designed such items as the attraction poster for "it's a small world" and the Walt Disney World fun map.

Elmer Plummer was an animator who worked on such films as *The Three Caballeros*, *Dumbo*, and *Fantasia*. He went on to become a design specialist for WED Enterprises.

Ernie Prinzhorn was a design specialist for WED Enterprises who worked on the concept art for attractions at Walt Disney World, including the never-built Western River Expedition and Thunder Mesa.

Jefferds'
Mail Order Service
Sales Promotions
We Sell-Trade
Everything Under The Sun
Vince Jefferds
The Original Merchant Prince

VINCENT "VINCE" JEFFERDS began working for Disney's merchandising office in New York City in 1951. By 1960, he had moved to Burbank, California to head national merchandising operations. By 1967, he was Head of Marketing Services. In 1972, he was Vice President of Sales Promotions for Domestic and Foreign Divisions. Finally, he became Senior Vice President of Marketing, a position he held until he retired in 1983. Throughout his career at Disney, he helped to market Disney characters through toys, ice shows, and books, some of which he wrote himself.

Snap On Electric Co.
1% Inspiration
99% Perspiration
Wilbur K. Watt, President
Lou Tonarely, V.P.

WILBUR K. WATT was the name of the "electro-mechanical" man who was going to host a show in the proposed Edison Square expansion at Disneyland, sponsored by General Electric.

LOUIS "LOU" TONARELY was an electrical engineer at WED Enterprises.

VINCE JEFFERDS
The *Original* Merchant Prince

1% INSPIRATION
99% PERSPIRATION

WILLIAM & SHARON LUND
GALLERY
EXHIBITING ONLY AUTHENTIC WORKS OF ART
GENUINE ANTIQUES
SELECTED BY VICTORIA, BRADFORD & MICHELLE

WILLIAM "BILL" S. LUND married Walt's daughter Sharon in 1963. He was a real estate developer, and helped build Walt Disney World.

SHARON MAE DISNEY LUND was born in 1936, and was Walt and Lillian's adopted daughter. She was an officer of Retlaw Enterprises, which Walt established to help further his family's personal business interests. She served on the Disney Board of Directors.

VICTORIA BROWN LUND was Sharon's daughter from her first marriage to Robert Borgfeldt Brown. The Victoria Lund Foundation operates in her name, which donates to the Boys and Girls Club of Phoenix, The Parkinson's Disease Foundation, and the Southwest College of Naturopathic Medicine's Healthy Kids Program at Arthur M. Hamilton Elementary School.

BRADFORD "BRAD" LUND is the son of Bill and Sharon.

MICHELLE LUND is the daughter of Bill and Sharon. She is twins with Brad.

DAUGHTERLAND MODELING AGENCY
WHAT EVERY YOUNG GIRL SHOULD KNOW!
INSTRUCTION IN THE ARTS & CRAFTS
BOB SEWELL   COUNSELOR
MALCOLM COBB   JACK FERGES
FRED JOERGER   MITZ NATSUME

J. ROBERT "BOB" SEWELL worked at museums, such as the Los Angeles Museum of Natural History, before doing contract work for The Walt Disney Company in the 1950s. He worked on the *True-Life Adventure* series, and the Grand Canyon Diorama for the Disneyland Railroad. He became a full-time employee at WED Enterprises in 1957. By 1960, he was Head of the Model Shop, and stayed in that position until he retired in 1981. He supervised the design and installation for many of the attractions at Disneyland, the Magic Kingdom, and Epcot.

MALCOLM COBB was originally an animator at Walt Disney Studios. He was once told to go through the animation cels and throw out the ones he thought wouldn't be worth anything. The rest were sold to the public. Malcolm was Bob Sewell's right-hand man and assistant in the model shop.

JACK FERGES worked in the model shop, and designed models for many famous attractions, such as the Haunted Mansion, Pirates of the Caribbean, and the never-built Museum of the Weird. He also formed the Tip-Top Club, which was for anybody over 6'6".

FRED JOERGER began his career at Disney designing backgrounds for Wathel Rogers' "Project Little Man." He went on to work with Wathel and Harriet Burns in the model shop, creating mockups for many Disneyland attractions. Fred was Disney's "resident rock expert," known for creating realistic rockwork. Though he retired in 1979, he returned as a field art director for Epcot.

MITZ NATSUME worked in the model shop at WED Enterprises.

WHAT EVERY YOUNG GIRL SHOULD KNOW

INSTRUCTION
ARTS & CRAFTS

Bob Sewell
Counselor
Malcolm Cobb

Jack Ferges
Fred Joerger
Mitz Natsume

The Main Street Diary
"True Tales of Inspiration"
Lee A. Cockerell
Editor-In-Chief

LEE A. COCKERELL had a long career in the hospitality industry before joining Disney in 1990 as Director of Food and Beverage and Quality Assurance for Disneyland Paris. In 1992, he took over as Senior Vice President of Resort Operations for Walt Disney World. In 1997, he became Executive Vice President of Operations for Walt Disney World.

B. Laval & Associates
"What We Build Together
Can Last Forever"

BRUCE LAVAL joined Disney in 1971 as an industrial engineer, before becoming Director of WED Enterprises' Florida Operations, and then General Manager of Future World at Epcot. He became Director of Project Development for Disney's Hollywood Studios, and then went on to become Executive Vice President of Operations Planning and Development for Walt Disney Attractions.

The Main Street Diary

"True Tales of Inspiration"

LEE A. COCKERELL

B. LAVAL
& ASSOCIATES

"What We Build Together Can Last Forever"

CENTRAL CASTING
JAMES PASSILLA
DIRECTOR
TOM EASTMAN
PAT VAUGHN
NO SHOES TOO LARGE TO FIT

JAMES "JIM" PASSILLA helped to run the original casting and training program for Walt Disney World. He was Head of Casting.

TOM EASTMAN helped to run the casting and training program. He was Head of the Walt Disney World arm of Disney University.

PAT VAUGHN helped to run the casting and training program. He was Head of Employee Relations.

SAWYER FENCE PAINTING CO
TOM NABBE
PROPRIETOR
ANAHEIM, CALIFORNIA
LAKE BUENA VISTA, FLORIDA

TOM NABBE started his career at Disneyland two days after opening day, selling *The Disneyland News* to Guests, at the ripe old age of 12. By 1956, Walt had hired him to play Tom Sawyer on the newly created Tom Sawyer Island. Tom outgrew the role a few years later, and went on to manage some of the attractions. He moved to Florida in 1971 to become Transportation Supervisor for the Monorail System, and from there went on to help open Disneyland Paris. He came back to Walt Disney World to become Manager of Distribution Services.

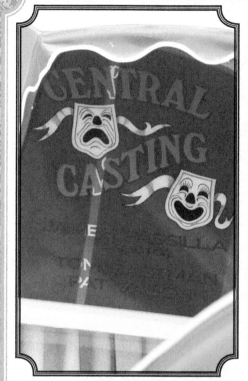

Buena Vista
Magic Lantern Slides
Treat Your Friends To Our Special Tricks
Yale Gracey
Bud Martin
Ken O'Brien
Wathel Rogers

YALE GRACEY was originally a writer and layout artist for many Disney films, including *Fantasia* and *The Three Caballeros*. After moving to WED Enterprises, he became a special effects wizard. He helped create some of the iconic effects in Pirates of the Caribbean and the Haunted Mansion.

WILLIAM BUD "BILL" MARTIN was an art director and set designer for WED Enterprises. He helped to develop many of the special effects used in Disney attractions.

KEN O'BRIEN was an animator for Walt Disney Studios before moving over to WED Enterprises. He worked on such attractions as Pirates of the Caribbean, The Hall of Presidents, Country Bear Jamboree, and World of Motion.

WATHEL ROGERS started as an animator at Walt Disney Studios in 1939 before moving to WED Enterprises in 1954. Because of his skill in the model shop, Wathel was asked by Walt to construct "Project Little Man," a nine-inch figure of a moving man, which was the prototype of early Audio-Animatronics. His groundbreaking achievements with the sixteenth President for Great Moments with Mr. Lincoln for the 1964-1965 New York World's Fair earned him the title of Mr. Audio-Animatronics. He spearheaded many of Imagineering's research and development projects, and became the first field art director of Walt Disney World.

Hyperion Film & Camera Exchange
World's Largest Film Library
Screenings daily at 4 p.m.
Dick Pfahler Bill Bosche Bob Gibeaut
Jack Boyd McLaren Stewart

Dick Pfahler was Head of Studio Operations. He worked on some of the films that are seen at Walt Disney World.

Bill Bosche was originally a sketch artist, but later became a writer for film and television projects, eventually working on scripting films for Walt Disney World.

Bob Gibeaut was originally Head of the Studio Editorial Department before coming Vice President of Studio Operations.

Jack Boyd was an animator for some of Disney's films before becoming a writer for Walt Disney World's film projects.

McLaren Stewart worked as a layout artist for the animation department. He moved over to work on film and television projects, such as *Walt Disney's Wonderful World of Color*. He also worked on Walt Disney World's film projects.

Burbank House of Graphics
Complete Catalogue of Brochures for Every Occasion
C. Robert Moore Norm Noceti
Layouts on Request

C. Robert "Bob" Moore started as an apprentice animator in 1940, and worked on such films as *Dumbo*, *The Reluctant Dragon*, and *The Three Caballeros*. During World War II, Bob was drafted to a special unit dedicated to producing animated training films for the US Navy. In 1951, he became Head of the Studio's Publicity and Art Department, helping to draw movie posters, logos, and the mascot of the 1984 Olympics.

Norm Noceti was a cartoonist and artist for Walt Disney Productions, contributing to comic books, story books, and layout design.

AMPLIFICATION CO
GORDON WILLIAMS
ED CHISHOLM

GORDON WILLIAMS developed many of the sound effects used throughout Disneyland and Walt Disney World, most notably in the Haunted Mansion. He also assisted with programming Audio-Animatronics.

ED CHISHOLM was a manufacturing mechanical engineer for WED Enterprises.

MANUSCRIPTS AND MELODRAMAS
F.X. ATENCIO
AL BERTINO
MARTY SKLAR

FRANCIS XAVIER "X" ATENCIO pennned two of the most famous Disney attraction songs of all time: *Yo Ho (A Pirate's Life For Me)* with composer George Bruns, and *Grim Grinning Ghosts* with composer Buddy Baker.

ALBERT "AL" BERTINO worked on many of Disney's animated films, such as *Pinocchio* and *Fantasia*. He was also instrumental in creating some of Disneyland's most memorable attractions, such as the Haunted Mansion, America Sings, Mr. Toad's Wild Ride, and Country Bear Jamboree. Al was the inspiration for Big Al in Country Bear Jamboree.

MARTIN A. "MARTY" SKLAR started working in Disneyland's publicity department before he had graduated from UCLA. Marty joined WED Enterprises in 1961 to work on the attractions for the 1964-1965 New York World's Fair. In 1974, Marty became Creative Lead of Imagineering, and helped develop Disney theme parks around the world for the next 35 years.

HOLLYWOOD PUBLISHING CO.

This Window is for atmosphere only, and does not pay tribute to anyone.

DRAUGHTING CORPORATION
DOUG CAYNE   DELINEATOR
OUR MOTTO
"A STRAIGHT LINE IS THE FIRST RULE"
ASSOCIATES
JOE KRAMER   GEORGE WINDRUM   RON BOWMAN
GLENN DURFLINGER   DON HOLMQUIST
DICK KLINE   GEORGE NELSON

DOUG CAYNE was a project designer for WED Enterprises.

JOE KRAMER was an architect for WED Enterprises.

GEORGE WINDRUM was in charge of show set design for WED Enterprises.

RON BOWMAN was in charge of the architectural drafting department for WED Enterprises.

GLENN DURFLINGER started with Disney in 1965, leading teams of architects and engineers to design many of the most beloved attractions. He was Assistant Project Designer for Magic Kingdom's Fantasyland, and went on to become Director of Architecture for Epcot.

DON HOLMQUIST was an architect for WED Enterprises.

RICHARD "DICK" KLINE started his architectural career at Disney by helping design Club 33, and Walt and Roy's proposed New Orleans Square apartment, on what was supposed to be a two-week contract. He went on to work on River Country, the Magic Kingdom's Adventureland, Epcot, and the never-built Mineral King Ski Resort. He also contributed designs for Tokyo Disneyland and Disneyland Paris.

GEORGE NELSON was an architect for WED Enterprises.

Dreamers & Doers
Development Co.
Roy O. Disney
Chairman
"If we can Dream it - we can Do it!"

ROY OLIVER DISNEY was Walt Disney's older brother, partner, and co-founder of The Walt Disney Company. While Walt took the spotlight and came up with the ideas, Roy was the behind-the-scenes man who did everything he could to make sure his brother's dreams, from the animated films to the theme parks, were financially possible. He became the unofficial CEO in 1929, but was not officially given the title until 1968. He shared the title of Chairman of the Board with Walt. Roy postponed his retirement after Walt's death to oversee the construction of the Florida Project. He renamed the project from Disney World to Walt Disney World to pay tribute to his brother.

General Joe's Building Permits
General Joe's
Racontuer

GENERAL WILLIAM EVERETT "JOE" POTTER graduated from the United States Military Academy at West Point in 1928. He got a degree in civil engineering from Massachusetts Institute of Technology in 1933. He went on to serve as Governor of the Panama Canal Zone from 1956 to 1960. Joe met Walt at the 1964-1965 New York World's Fair, and played an important role in the construction of Walt Disney World. He is often credited as being the one who built the underground utilities and other infrastructure that help the resort run smoothly.

CONSTRUCTION COMPANY
STATE LICENSED   BONDED
SCHEDULES CHANGED   WHILE-YOU-WAIT
GENERAL CONTRACTOR
PETER MARKHAM   ENGINEER
BILL IRWIN   FIELD CALCULATIONS
LARRY REISER   SYNCHRONIZER
FRANCIS STANEK   PROGNOSTICATIONS
DAN DINGMAN   RECKONING

PETER MARKHAM was Chief Executive Engineer for the Buena Vista Construction Company, which was the general contractor for the construction of Walt Disney World.

WILLIAM "BILL" IRWIN was a chief executive of the Buena Vista Construction Company.

LAWRENCE "LARRY" REISER was a chief executive of the Buena Vista Construction Company.

FRANCIS "FRANK" STANEK was a chief executive of the Buena Vista Construction Company.

DANIEL B. "DAN" DINGMAN was a chief executive of the Buena Vista Construction Company.

TOWN SQUARE TAILORS
TAILORS TO THE PRESIDENTS
BOB PHELPS
PROP.

ROBERT "BOB" PHELPS got his start making costumes for movies. He joined Disney in 1967 to help create some of the iconic costumes that Cast Members have worn over the years. He was in charge of costuming for the Magic Kingdom, Epcot, Tokyo Disneyland, and Disneyland Paris. He costumed the original Audio-Animatronic figures in The Hall of Presidents. Bob was made Vice President of Costuming, and he retired in 1995.

BILL IRWIN
FIELD CALCULATIONS

GENERAL
CONTRACTOR

PETE MARKHAM
ENGINEER

FRANCIS STANEK
PROGNOSTICATIONS

LARRY REISER
RETRORIZER

DAN DINGMAN
RECKONING

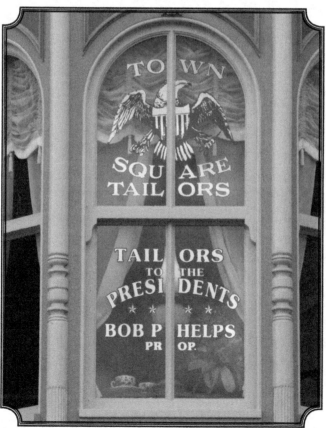

TOWN
SQUARE
TAILORS

TAILORS
TO THE
PRESIDENTS
* * *   * * *
BOB PHELPS
PROP.

Fashions By John
Dressmaking
Hemstitching & Picoting
Tom Peirce Orpha Harryman Ken Creekmore
Alyja Paskevicius John Keehne

Tom Peirce was a costume designer at Disneyland, who later worked under Bob Phelps to help design Walt Disney World's Cast Member and Audio-Animatronic costumes.

Orpha Harryman was one of the original costume managers at Walt Disney World.

Ken Creekmore was one of the original costume managers at Walt Disney World.

Alyja Paskevicius Kalinich designed costumes as a sketch artist at Disneyland for years, before moving on to do the same at Walt Disney World and Tokyo Disneyland Resort.

John Keehne was one of the original members of the Disney Costume Team. He was Supervisor of the Wardrobe Department, and was later promoted to Manager of Costuming and Wardrobe Issue. He is the John referred to in "Fashions By John."

This Window used to contain six names. A former Show Quality Monitor was building an index of all the Windows on Main Street. When researching this Window, he found information on the five names that currently are on the Window without much difficulty, but came up short on the sixth. He wrote to the corporate personnel archives to ask what that person did for the Company. They replied that he had worked for Disney, but only for about four months. The mystery became clearer when it was discovered that this sixth person had worked in the Sign shop and his job had included painting and touching up the Windows on Main Street. Apparently, he thought that five names didn't balance well when they were split into two and three, so had inserted his own name to make it look more balanced.

FASHIONS
BY
JOHN

DRESSMAKING

HEMSTITCHING
& PICOTING

TOM PEIRCE   KEN CHEEKMORE
ORPHA HARRYMAN   ALYJA PASKEVICIUS
                         JOHN KEEHNE

Tokyo Disneyland

Miss Abigail Potter
Dressmaker Day Dresses
Traveling Suits Party Gowns

Abigail Potter worked on the architecture of Cinderella Castle at Tokyo Disneyland.

Oriental Land Co. Ltd.

Oriental Land Company is a leisure and tourism corporation in Japan. They financed Tokyo Disneyland after they approached Disney with the idea in 1980. They pay Disney for licenses to have characters and other likenesses in the Park.

Alice Bluebonnet
Hats for Every Occasion

Alice Bluebonnet is a character from the *Johnnie Fedora and Alice Bluebonnet* segment of *Make Mine Music*. Alice is a blue bonnet.

Main Str. Tailor

This Window is for atmosphere only, and does not pay tribute to anyone.

The Double Check Co.
"A Penny Saved Is A Penny Earned"
B. Franklin

Benjamin Franklin was one of the Founding Fathers of the United States. He famously once said "A Penny Saved Is A Penny Earned."

Four Corners
Travel Agency
Reservations by Cable
Anywhere in the World

This Window is for atmosphere only, and does not pay tribute to anyone.

Branchoff & Willow
Tree Surgeons
We grow 'em
You show 'em

Daniel Branchoff helped design the landscaping for Tokyo Disneyland and Disneyland Paris.

Brian Willow worked with Daniel Branchoff, designing the landscaping for Tokyo Disneyland.

Mayken Offre
Real Estate
Investments
"A Friend in Deeds is a Friend Indeed"

Mayken Offre is not a real person, but a play on words for "make an offer."

Insurance
Life Fire

This Window is for atmosphere only, and does not pay tribute to anyone.

Law Offices
D. Fense   O. Fense
Partners
Fense Bros.
Attorneys-At-Law

D. Fense is not a real person, but a play on words for "defense."

O. Fense is not a real person, but a play on words for "offense."

Detective Agency
"We Never Sleep"

This Window is for atmosphere only, and does not pay tribute to anyone.

W.B. Water Works
Let Us Solve Your Plumbing Problems

This Window is for atmosphere only, and does not pay tribute to anyone.

I Super Structures Inc.
Engineers & Associates

This Window is for atmosphere only, and does not pay tribute to anyone.

SNAP ON ELECTRIC CO.
1% INSPIRATION
99% PERSPIRATION
WILBUR K. WATT, PRESIDENT

WILBUR K. WATT was the name of the "electro-mechanical" man who was going to host a show in the proposed Edison Square expansion at Disneyland, sponsored by General Electric.

DREAMS UNLIMITED DEVELOPMENT CO.
TOSHIO KAGAMI
PRINCIPAL
EXPANDING THE MAGIC FROM LAND TO SEA
GRANDER VISIONS ARE OUR SPECIALTY

TOSHIO KAGAMI is Representative Director, Chairman, and CEO of Oriental Land Company, and President of Tokyo Disneyland Resort. "Expanding the Magic from Land to Sea" refers to the names of the two Parks at Tokyo Disneyland Resort: Tokyo Disneyland and Tokyo DisneySea.

ROY OLIVER DISNEY was Walt Disney's older brother, partner, and co-founder of The Walt Disney Company. He became the unofficial CEO in 1929, but was not officially given the title until 1968.

WALTER ELIAS DISNEY is the man who made the dream called Disneyland a reality. Walt's fingerprints can be seen all over the Disney Parks today, even though he did not survive to see all of them open.

POLLY HARRINGTON is the name of the aunt of the titular character in the 1960 Disney film *Pollyanna*. It is also the name of the town that Pollyanna goes to live in.

This Window is for atmosphere only, and does not pay tribute to anyone.

Office of Legendary Creations
Having the Vision and Daring to Do
Making the Magic of Dreams Come True
Masatomo Takahashi
Founder

MASATOMO TAKAHASHI was the founder of Oriental Land Company. He is considered the "Walt Disney of Japan" for his vision of bringing the Park to his country.

FAMILY MORTGAGE TRUST
MUNICIPAL STOCKS AND BONDS
LOANS AND DEDENTURES
INTEREST LOW
TERMS FAVORABLE
NO DELAY

This Window is for atmosphere only, and does not pay tribute to anyone.

VISIONARY MANAGEMENT
YOU'VE GOT THE VISION
WE'VE GOT THE TEAM
YOU BRING THE PROJECT
WE'LL BUILD YOUR DREAM
JIM CORA
PROPRIETOR

JIM CORA started as a part-time Cast Member in 1958, and climbed through the ranks in no time at all. He helped open Walt Disney World in 1971, and then came back to Disneyland in 1974 to become Director of Operations for Fantasyland and Tomorrowland. He helped with management duties at Tokyo Disneyland before working on the plan for Disneyland Paris. He was made President of Disneyland International in 1995, and then took over as Chairman in 1999.

DRESSMAKING
HEMSTITCHING
PICOTING
ALTERATIONS

This Window is for atmosphere only, and does not pay tribute to anyone.

GLENDALE ACADEMY FOR AIR
NATURAL GAS BALLOON RIDES
FLYING INSTRUCTION
WING WALKING
EXHIBITIONS
AERIAL DRAMATICS &
DAREDEVIL ACTS

GLENDALE in California is where Imagineering headquarters is located.

DR. SEER
PREDICTIONS
PRESTIDIGITATIONS

DR. SEER is not a real person, but a reference to a seer: someone who can see the future.

GRAND ORDER OF THE GOLDEN BEARS
FRATERNAL HALL
LODGE MEETINGS EVERY THURSDAY

This Window is for atmosphere only, and does not pay tribute to anyone.

THE CAT'S EYE GALLERY
EXHIBITING ONLY AUTHENTIC WORKS OF ART
GENUINE ANTIQUES

This Window is for atmosphere only, and does not pay tribute to anyone.

Baron Tonn
Music Academy
Voice Training
Cello Piano Violin

Baron Tonn is not a real person, but a play on words for "baritone."

Graphic Arts Studio
Latest Artistic Principles Employed

This Window is for atmosphere only, and does not pay tribute to anyone.

T. Hook's
Custom Corsettes

T. Hook is not a real person, but a play on words for "tee hook," an item which ladies used for putting corsets on during the 19th century.

Johnny Fedora
Hatmaker

Johnnie Fedora is a character from the *Johnnie Fedora and Alice Bluebonnet* segment of *Make Mine Music*. Johnnie is a fedora. His name is spelled incorrectly on the Window.

Hollywood Publishing Co.
Plays   Screenplays
Sheet Music

This Window is for atmosphere only, and does not pay tribute to anyone.

LACEMAKER
FINE HAND MADE LACES
IMPORTED FRENCH & AUSTRIAN LACES

This Window is for atmosphere only, and does not pay tribute to anyone.

WE'VE GOT TALENT!
TOKYO DISNEYLAND
CASTING AGENCY
WALTER ELIAS DISNEY
FOUNDER & DIRECTOR EMERITUS
"IT TAKES PEOPLE TO MAKE THE DREAM A REALITY"

WALTER ELIAS DISNEY is the name on this Window, although it is actually a tribute to all Tokyo Disneyland Resort Cast Members, past and present.

Walter E. Disney & Associates
Design & Masterplanning
If it can be imagined...it can be created

Walter Elias Disney is the man who made the dream called Disneyland a reality. Walt's fingerprints can be seen all over the Disney Parks today, even though he did not survive to see all of them open.

Disneyland Paris

DANIEL BRANCHOFF
TREE SURGEON

DANIEL BRANCHOFF helped design the landscaping for Tokyo Disneyland and Disneyland Paris.

CONRADS
SEEDS & GARDEN SUPPLIES
GROWERS
VEGETABLES
TREES
SEE OUR CATALOG

JERRY CONRAD was responsible for some of the landscaping and gardening of Disneyland Paris.

CREME DE LA CREME
COOKING COLLEGE
SPECIALIZING IN THE ART OF FINE
FRENCH CUISINE
INSTRUCTORS
HOWARD GEVERTZ   DAVE VERMEULEN

HOWARD GEVERTZ was Director of Food and Beverage for Disneyland Paris when it opened. He was involved in the conception, planning, production, and opening of all the restaurants and snack carts for the resort.

DAVE VERMEULEN started his career at Disney by serving ice cream at Disneyland. He moved up throughout the years, assisting Howard with the food and beverage department at Disneyland Paris. He became Vice President of Resort Operations for Hong Kong Disneyland, and then Vice President and Executive Managing Director for Walt Disney Attractions in Japan.

NET, GROSS,
FORSGREN & GREEN
COUNSELORS OF INVESTMENT
JOHN FORSGREN   JUDSON GREEN
"PUT YOUR MONEY WHERE THE MOUSE IS"

JOHN FORSGREN was Vice President and Treasurer of Disneyland Paris before its opening, and went on to become Senior Vice President and Chief Financial Officer of the Park until 1994.

JUDSON GREEN was Chief Financial Officer of The Walt Disney Company, until he was promoted to President of Disney Theme Parks and Resorts in 1991. He helped to expand the Company through the Disney Cruise Line, Tokyo Disneyland, and Disneyland Paris.

Main Street Volunteer Fire Department
Putting Out Fires Before They Start
Jeff Burton   Tony Catton
Rick Girdley   Paul La France
David Todd   John Verity

Jeff Burton was a project manager at Imagineering, who worked on Epcot, Disney's Hollywood Studios, and Disneyland Paris. He was Project Director for Main Street at Disneyland Paris.

Tony Catton was Project Director for Discoveryland at Disneyland Paris.

Richard "Rick" Girdley worked on design, engineering, and project management during the construction of Disneyland Paris. He was responsible for the infrastructure and area development of the resort.

Paul La France was Project Director for Adventureland at Disneyland Paris. He was Head of Design and Construction for Walt Disney Studios Park, and Head of Construction of Hong Kong Disneyland. Before leaving Disney, he was Project Vice President of Imagineering.

David Todd started as a part-time Cast Member at the Magic Kingdom in 1971, before moving to Imagineering to work on Epcot. After leaving to work on the 1984 Olympics, he returned in 1987 as Project Director for Fantasyland at Disneyland Paris. Between 1996 and 2001, he was Project Executive for an expansion at Disneyland Resort that included Disney California Adventure, Downtown Disney, and Disney's Grand Californian Hotel & Spa. In 2004, he became President of Disneyland Paris Imagineering, where he headed a major expansion until early 2008. He left the Company in 2009.

John Verity was Project Manager for Frontierland at Disneyland Paris, Managing Director of Walt Disney Imagineering Hong Kong, and now serves as a project management Vice President of Imagineering.

CONDUCTED DAILY
MAIN STREET MARCHING BAND
LEADING THE PARADE SINCE 1884
CONDUCTORS
MICHAEL EISNER   FRANK WELLS
"WE WORK WHILE YOU WHISTLE"

MICHAEL D. EISNER was brought in as Chairman and CEO in 1984 to help revitalize The Walt Disney Company. Working with Frank Wells, the two men helped turn Disney around and back into the powerhouse entertainment machine it once was, saving it from being bought off by other companies. When Wells passed away in 1994, Eisner absorbed his roles as well, taking on many of Disney's problems himself, expanding the Disney Company at a rapid rate. Eventually, at the behest of the Board of Directors, he resigned in 2005.

FRANK G. WELLS was The Walt Disney Company's President and Chief Operating Officer. He worked closely with Chairman and Chief Executive Officer Michael Eisner. He passed away in a helicopter crash in 1994.

FITZPATRICKS FINE TAILORING
A FIT FOR EVERY OCCASION
ROBERT FITZPATRICK
PROPRIETOR

ROBERT FITZPATRICK was Chairman of Disneyland Paris from March 1987 until April 1992, where he oversaw the creation and production of the Park.

"INTENSE" TRAVELLING PRODUCTIONS
ERIC VAN DIJK   DIRECTOR
JEAN-LUC CHOPLIN   CASTING
TOM JACOBSON   COSTUMES
THE GREATEST SHOWS ON EARTH ARE IN TENTS

ERIC VAN DIJK was Guest Entry Sequence Show Producer for Disneyland Paris.

JEAN-LUC CHOPLIN was Vice President of Entertainment for Disneyland Paris. He moved to California in 1995 to become Vice President of Creative Development for Imagineering.

TOM JACOBSON worked on some of the costumes for Disneyland Paris. He was also a production manager on several Disney films.

BIXBY BROTHERS
FINE ACCESSORIES
FOR LADIES & GENTLEMEN

THE BIXBY BROTHERS are not based on real people. This Window is for atmosphere only.

Attorneys At Law
Stephen Juge
Andrew Hibbert
Joe Shapiro
Patents Wills Claims
No Claim No Settlement Too Small

Stephen Juge worked in the legal department for Disneyland Paris during its opening, and then became Senior Vice President and General Counsel of Walt Disney International for Europe.

Andrew P. Hibbert was Vice President of Legal Affairs and Deputy General Counsel for Disneyland Paris.

Joseph "Joe" Shapiro started working for Disney in 1985 as the chief negotiator with the French government on Disneyland Paris. He was General Counsel for the Park and soon rose to become Head of the Legal Department. He was known to pursue companies who used Disney characters without permission.

Dick Nunis
Consultant At Large
World Famous Psychic
Predicts Your Future
Knows Your Past
Open House

Richard "Dick" Nunis was hired in 1955 to help with training Disneyland employees. He was promoted to Attractions Supervisor, and later, as Chairman of the Park Operations Committee, he was instrumental in helping get the Florida Project off the ground. He was promoted to Executive Vice President of Walt Disney World and Disneyland in 1971, and served as member of the Board of Directors from 1981 to 1999.

Xavier's Dance Studio
Tap
Dance
Ballet
The Art Of Latin Dance
Beginner and Advanced Classes

Francis Xavier "X" Atencio joined Disney as an inbetweener on *Fantasia* in 1938. Atencio continued to work as an animator until 1965, when he moved over to WED Enterprises. His first assignment was to work on the design of the Primeval World Diorama for the Disneyland Railroad. After that, Walt asked him to write the dialogue and lyrics for two of their latest attractions. Atencio had never written before, but he was able to pen two of the most famous Disney attraction songs of all time: *Yo Ho (A Pirate's Life For Me)* with composer George Bruns, and *Grim Grinning Ghosts* with composer Buddy Baker. Atencio went on to become the in-house scriptwriter for many of the attractions that WED developed. Every so often you can hear a tap lesson coming from the Window.

Chas. Packett and Company
Using the finest leathers and upholsteries
Durable Practical
Steamer Trunks
Carpet Bags
Satchels
See Our Patented Travel Case
All Purpose

Charles Packett is not a real person, but his surname is a play on words for "pack it," an instruction to pack a trunk or bag.

OPEN SINCE '92
DISNEYLAND PARK
CASTING AGENCY
"IT TAKES PEOPLE TO MAKE THE DREAM A REALITY"
WALTER ELIAS DISNEY
FOUNDER & DIRECTOR EMERITUS

WALTER ELIAS DISNEY is the name on this Window, although it is actually a tribute to all Disneyland Paris Cast Members, past and present.

MIRACLE CONSTRUCTION CO.
BILL GAIR
BOB SMITH
BUD STACY
"IF IT'S ON TIME, IT'S A MIRACLE"

BILL GAIR was the first executive to relocate to France for Disneyland Paris. He worked for The Walt Disney Company for over 30 years, holding executive positions in operations, construction, and more before becoming Director of Facilities Management for Disneyland Paris. He would later become Vice President of Resort Operations for Tokyo Disneyland.

BOB SMITH helped to design the layout, and oversaw the construction, of the stores at Disneyland Paris.

BUD STACY was an engineer during the creation of Epcot, and oversaw part of the construction of Disneyland Paris.

J. Norworth & A. Von Tilzer
Songwriters
Take Me Out to the Ball Game
Now Available in Sheet Music

Jack Norworth wrote the lyrics to *Take Me Out to the Ball Game* in 1908.

Albert Von Tilzer wrote the music for *Take Me Out to the Ball Game* in 1908.

These Windows are located above Casey's Corner, which is baseball-themed.

Victoria's Home Style Restaurant
Boarding House   Rooms to Let

This Window is for atmosphere only, and does not pay tribute to anyone. However, every so often you can hear a man washing himself from the Window.

Society of Arts and Craftsmen
Ron Esposito   Skip Lange   John Olsen
We'll Make Your Molehill into a Mountain

Ron Esposito was responsible for many of the color schemes at Disneyland Paris. He also worked on Walt Disney Studios Park as an art director.

Skip Lange was a field art director for Disneyland Paris. He also worked on rock fabrication, set installation, and facade materials and creation. He would go on to become Executive Production Vice President at Imagineering, and work on Hong Kong Disneyland.

John Olsen worked in the model shop at Imagineering, and helped with the art direction of Disneyland Paris. He played one of the brothers in the "Two Brothers" sequence in The American Adventure at Epcot and Great Moments with Mr. Lincoln at Disneyland.

MAIN STREET
SCHOOL OF CHARM
INSTRUCTORS
STEVE LEWELLING
HANNY VARMA
MALCOLM ROSS
WE'LL MAKE YOUR GUESTS FEEL LIKE VIPS

STEVE LEWELLING worked in design, development, operations, and human resources for Disneyland Paris, eventually receiving the title of Vice President of Operations for Disney's international theme park division.

HANNY VARMA worked in human resources underneath Steve Lewelling for the opening of Disneyland Paris.

MALCOLM ROSS was Vice President of Disneyland Paris during its construction and held onto that title until 1995. From there, he became Vice President of Disney's Hollywood Studios, until he became Vice President of Resort Operations for Walt Disney World in 2000.

MRS. TWIDDLE'S
SECRETARIAL SERVICES
TYPING

This Window is for atmosphere only, and does not pay tribute to anyone.

CHASTAIN
DESIGN COMPANY
OF GLENDALE
BUDGETS AND SCHEDULES MET
GUARANTEED

CHASTAIN is the name of a building at Walt Disney Imagineering in Glendale, California.

MARTIN A. "MARTY" SKLAR joined WED Enterprises in 1961 to work on the attractions for the 1964-1965 New York World's Fair. In 1974, Marty became Creative Lead of Imagineering, and retired on July 17, 2009.

TONY BAXTER joined Imagineering in 1970. He was made Senior Vice President of Imagineering, and held that title until he retired in 2013.

MAIN STREET GAZETTE
ADVERTISERS WELCOMED
PUBLICITY EXPERTS AT YOUR SERVICE!
JEAN-MARIE GERBEAUX
TOM ELROD

JEAN-MARIE GERBEAUX was Vice President of Communications at Disneyland Paris.

THOMAS R. "TOM" ELROD joined Disney in 1973 as a senior representative for advertising and promotion at Walt Disney World. He soon became Director of Marketing in 1976, and then Senior Vice President of Marketing in 1981, and finally President of Marketing and Entertainment in 1992. He oversaw the opening of Epcot, Disney's Hollywood Studios, and Disneyland Paris. He was also one of the executives responsible for the "I'm going to Disney World/Disneyland!" campaign.

MAIN STREET GAZETTE
CLASSIFIED DEPARTMENT
WE DEMONSTRATE THE HIGHEST REGARD FOR TRUTH IN
ADVERTISING
HONEST
MARK FEARY
RON KOLLEN

MARK FEARY was Marketing Director for Disneyland. He became Vice President of Marketing, and helped with the design and construction of Disneyland Paris. He later moved back to California to work as Vice President of Sales for Disneyland.

RON KOLLEN was Advertising Director of Disneyland Paris until 1995.

CAROLWOOD PACIFIC
BUSINESS OFFICE
THE BIGGEST LITTLE RAILROAD IN THE WORLD
FAIR WEATHER ROUTE

THE CAROLWOOD PACIFIC RAILROAD was a 1/8 scale railroad which ran around Walt Disney's Holmby Hills home.

Doctor's Office
Robt. Sherwood M.D.
General Medicine and Surgery

Dr. Robert Sherwood was a Marceline, Missouri resident who was the first person to pay Walt Disney for a drawing.

Nellie Bly
Travel Agency
Rail Land Sea
"Book Passage Around the World or Around the Corner"

Elizabeth Jane Cochrane was an American journalist who used the pen name Nellie Bly. She was known for her record-breaking trip around the world in 72 days.

We Know How To Let Off Steam
Euro Disneyland Railroad
Main Street, U.S.A.
Orlando Ferrante   Wayne Jackson
Dave Spencer   Tim Kelley
Stokers, Brakemen & Engineers

Orlando Ferrante was a 40-year veteran of The Walt Disney Company, having overseen the engineering, design production, and installation of Disney Parks all around the world.

Wayne Jackson helped to develop and build many of the Audio-Animatronic figures for Disneyland, Walt Disney World, and Tokyo DisneySea. He was Director of Ride and Show Production for Disneyland Paris.

David "Dave" Spencer was Executive Director of Research and Development at Imagineering.

Tim Kelley worked on Autopia at Disneyland, where he created the prototype of the Mark VII car. He would later work on the original version of Test Track at Epcot as a mechanical engineer.

Top Brass
Band Instruments
Philippe Bourguignon   Steve Burke
Lessons and Fine Tuning
"And the Band Plays On"

Philippe Bourguignon joined The Walt Disney Company in 1990 to work on various projects at Disneyland before relocating to Paris, where he became Chairman and CEO of Euro Disney S.C.A., the parent company of Disneyland Paris. He also became Executive Vice President of The Walt Disney Company (Europe) S.C.A., where he oversaw all of the Company's dealings and activities in Europe.

Steve Burke joined The Walt Disney Company in 1986, and quickly became the protégé of Frank Wells. In 1992, he became President and Chief Operating Officer of Euro Disney S.C.A.

5 Cents A Foot
Your Name Here

This Window is for atmosphere only, and does not pay tribute to anyone.

M Jones Electronics
Edison Talking Machines
Cinemascope

Merlin Jones is a fictional character played by Tommy Kirk in the 1964 film *The Misadventures of Merlin Jones*.

Evans and Markham Advertising
Products Tested
Advertisements Created

Spin Evans is a fictional character played by Tim Considine in *Spin and Marty*, a serial from the 1950s version of *The Mickey Mouse Club*. Spin was the most popular boy at the Triple R Ranch, although his family was poor.

Martin "Marty" Markham is a fictional character played by David Stollery in *Spin and Marty*, a serial from the 1950s version of *The Mickey Mouse Club*. Marty was a rich orphan who wound up at the Triple R Ranch.

DIGBY'S MESSENGER SERVICE
RAPID DELIVERIES

DIGBY POPHAM is a fictional character played by Michael J. Pollard in the 1963 film *Summer Magic*.

PIANO LESSONS
UPSTAIRS
ASK FOR SARA

This Window is for atmosphere only, and does not pay tribute to anyone. However, every so often you can hear someone practicing piano from the Window.

MRS. CINCH'S CUSTOM CORSETS
FASHIONABLE STYLES
PROPER SUPPORT
GENUINE WHALEBONE STAYS

MRS. CINCH is not a real person, but a reference to cincher, a belt worn with a corset to make the waist smaller.

Top Notch Talent Agency
TNT
Jugglers Singers
Musicians Comedians
Actors

This Window is for atmosphere only, and does not pay tribute to anyone. However, every so often you can hear a dog barking from the Window.

Mr. "Lucky"
Tailor Shop
Home Laundry Service
Mah-Jongg Parlor Upstairs
Alterations
Hand Washing

This Window is for atmosphere only, and does not pay tribute to anyone. However, every so often you could hear a Mah-Jongg session from the Window.

The Third Eye
Detective Agency
John Larsen
Gerard Degonse

John Larsen was a creative designer and director for Disneyland Paris.

Gerald Degonse was Vice President, Financial Manager, and Secretary General of Disneyland Paris from 1989 until 1994.

Town Square Taxidermy
Sam Hutchins   Claudine Reynes
"If It's Stuffed, We Sell it."

Sam Hutchins worked for The Walt Disney Company for many years before becoming Director of Merchandising for Disneyland Paris. He was also in charge of merchandising for Tokyo Disneyland.

Claudine Reynes worked in the merchandising department for Disneyland Paris.

Matchmaking & Counselor of Marriages
Frank Halard   Eric Westin   Jon Winder

Frank Halard was Director of Partnership, in charge of strategy and negotiation of corporate partnerships for Disneyland Paris.

Eric Westin worked for Imagineering in the 1970s, but left soon after to work for Lucasfilm. He returned in 1987 to become Vice President and General Manager of the Creative Group for Disneyland Paris.

Jon Winder was Vice President of Marketing for Disneyland Paris.

Two Brothers Inc.
Dreamers & Doers
"If we can Dream it we can Do it!"
Roy O. Disney   Walt E. Disney
Founders and Partners

Roy Oliver Disney was Walt Disney's older brother, partner, and co-founder of The Walt Disney Company.

Walter Elias Disney is the man who made the dream called Disneyland a reality. Walt's fingerprints can be seen all over the Disney Parks today, even though he did not survive to see all of them open.

ROY O. DISNEY

WALT E. DISNEY

BIG DEAL
GENERAL SUPPLIERS
PAUL MULLÉE
HERB SCHLEY
"IF WE DON'T HAVE IT, NEITHER DO YOU!"

PAUL MULLÉE was a developer who helped obtain the local supplies needed to construct Disneyland Paris.

HERB SCHLEY was a developer who helped supply building materials for Disneyland Paris during its construction.

PORTRAITS BY M. BRADY
WEDDINGS GRADUATIONS
A PORTRAIT TO SHARE
A KEEPSAKE TO TREASURE

MATTHEW BRADY was a famous photographer around the time of the US Civil War. The Window was thematically linked to the shop originally below it, Town Square Photography.

THE NEWEST RELEASES
THE LATEST PERFORMERS
GRAMOPHONE
UPTOWN RECORDING CO.

This Window is for atmosphere only, and does not pay tribute to anyone.

Second Opinion
Surgical Practice
Dr. Jim Cora
"Our Operations Will Keep You In Stitches"

Jim Cora started as a part-time Cast Member in 1958, and climbed through the ranks in no time at all. He helped open Walt Disney World in 1971, and then came back to Disneyland in 1974 to become Director of Operations for Fantasyland and Tomorrowland. He helped with management duties at Tokyo Disneyland before working on the plan for Disneyland Paris. He was made President of Disneyland International in 1995, and then took over as Chairman in 1999.

Language Lessons
Fred Benckenstein
Mickey Steinberg
"We'll teach you to speak American Guaranteed"

L.F. "Fred" Benckenstein was Vice President of Imagineering for Disneyland Paris during its construction, where he oversaw the day-to-day operations for its design team.

Mickey Steinberg was Chief Operating Officer for Imagineering during the construction of Disneyland Paris.

Kitty Hawk
Bicycle Shop
Closed
Flight Testing

Kitty Hawk is not a reference to a person, but rather to a place. Kitty Hawk, North Carolina, is where the Wright Brothers tested gliders before designing the first powered aircraft. They owned a bicycle shop and used bicycles for many of their early designs.

DEGELMANN
JANIER AND KANALLY
EFFICIENCY EXPERTS
THOR DEGELMANN PIERRE JANIER DAVID KANALLY
"ARE YOU READING THIS FAST ENOUGH?"

THOR DEGELMANN helped with the planning, concept, and human resources for Disneyland Paris.

PIERRE JANIER spent several months working at Walt Disney World before becoming Vice President of Human Resources for Disneyland Paris.

DAVID KANALLY worked in human resources for Disneyland Paris, specializing in the training programs at Disney University.

PYEWACKET CRUISE LINES
FOR A DAY YOU WILL TREASURE
BOOK A CRUISE THAT'S A "PLEASURE"
CAPT. ROY E. DISNEY

ROY EDWARD DISNEY was the son of Roy O. Disney, and Walt Disney's nephew. He began his career at Disney in 1951 as an assistant director and producer for the *True-Life Adventure* series. He was elected to the Board of Directors in 1967. Throughout the years, he was the spearhead of two separate "Save Disney" campaigns: the first ousted Ron Miller, and the second resulted in Michael Eisner's retirement. He is also notable for serving as a consultant for the Company for many years and being Director Emeritus for the Board of Directors. In his personal life, he was an avid sailor, and held many sailing speed records. Pyewacket is the name of Roy's boat, with which he set the Los Angeles to Honolulu monohull time record.

DEGELMANN
JANIER
KANALLY
**EFFICIENCY
EXPERTS**

Thor
Degelmann

Pierre
Janier

David
Kanally

"ARE YOU READING THIS

FAST ENOUGH ?

PYEWACKET

Cruise Lines

For a Day You Will Treasure

Book a Cruise That's a "Pleasure"

CAPT. ROY E. DISNEY

JEFF BURKE was Show Producer for Frontierland at Disneyland Paris. He was instrumental in the creation of Phantom Manor, Disneyland Paris' version of the Haunted Mansion.

TIM DELANEY was Show Producer for Discoveryland at Disneyland Paris. He had previously worked on Epcot, and would later go on to become Vice President of Design for Imagineering, where he worked on Hong Kong Disneyland.

TOM MORRIS was Show Producer for Fantasyland at Disneyland Paris, and would later become Vice President and Executive Producer of Hong Kong Disneyland.

CHRIS TIETZ was Show Producer for Adventureland at Disneyland Paris.

EDDIE SOTTO was Show Producer for Main Street at Disneyland Paris. He was later Senior Vice President of Concept Design at Walt Disney Imagineering.

E.S. BITZ is not a real person. It is often claimed that the "E.S." is a reference to Eddie Sotto, but according to Sotto himself, that is simply not true. However, every so often you can hear the sounds of the dentist's office from the Window.

Windows Elsewhere

Doc Holliday
Bones Set
Bullets Removed
Open Until Six O'clock
After Hours Inquire At Saloon

John Henry "Doc" Holliday was a famous gunfighter in the Old West, best known for his involvement in the fight at the O.K. Corral with Wyatt Earp. He was also a dentist. This Window is located by Last Chance Cafe in Frontierland.

Hong Kong Disneyland

Disney Brothers Co.
"The Original Dreamers and Doers"
Walter E. Disney
Roy O. Disney
Founders & Partners

Walter Elias Disney is the man who made the dream called Disneyland a reality. Walt's fingerprints can be seen all over the Disney Parks today, even though he did not survive to see all of them open.

Roy Oliver Disney was Walt Disney's older brother, partner, and co-founder of The Walt Disney Company. Roy was the behind-the-scenes man who did everything he could to make sure his brother's dreams were financially possible.

WPA
Works Progress Administration
Balancing Art and Commerce For A Better Tomorrow
Michael D. Eisner
Robert A. Iger

Michael D. Eisner was brought in as Chairman and CEO in 1984 to help revitalize The Walt Disney Company. Working with Frank Wells, the two men helped turn Disney around and back into the powerhouse entertainment machine it once was, saving it from being bought off by other companies.

Robert A. "Bob" Iger was President and Chief Operating Officer of ABC's parent company, Capital Cities/ABC, when Disney bought them in 1996. He stayed in that position until 1999, when he was named President of Walt Disney International. In 2000, he was named President and Chief Operating Officer of The Walt Disney Company. When Eisner resigned in 2005, he became CEO.

THE WONDERLAND QUINTET
AMUSEMENTS AND AMAZEMENTS
SKIP LANGE   ANN MALMLUND   KELLEY FORDE
LORI COLTRIN   TIM DELANEY
PRINCIPAL DESIGNERS

SKIP LANGE was a field art director for Disneyland Paris. He also worked on rock fabrication, set installation, and facade materials and creation. He would go on to become Executive Production Vice President at Imagineering, and work on Hong Kong Disneyland.

ANN MALMLUND is Director of Creative Development at Imagineering.

KELLEY FORDE is a Show Producer and Senior Director at Imagineering.

LORI COLTRIN is a Show Producer and Creative Director at Imagineering.

TIM DELANEY was Show Producer for Discoveryland at Disneyland Paris. He had previously worked on Epcot, and would later go on to become Vice President of Design for Imagineering, where he worked on Hong Kong Disneyland.

CARRIAGE BUILDERS
DON HILSEN   TOMMY JONES
RON HAMMING   JOEL FRITSCHE
"TAKING YOU FOR A RIDE SINCE 1865"

DON HILSEN started in ride engineering at Imagineering. He is currently their Senior Technical Director.

TOMMY JONES was Technical Director of Systems Engineering for Hong Kong Disneyland.

RON HAMMING is Ride Project Engineering Executive at Imagineering.

JOEL FRITSCHE is Executive Director of Ride Mechanical Engineering at Imagineering.

The Wonderland Quintet

AMUSEMENTS
AND
AMAZEMENTS

SKIP LANGE   KELLEY FORDE
ANN MALSBURY   TOM COLTRIN
        TIM
        DELANEY...

Principal Designers

CARRIAGE
BUILDERS

DON HILSEN
TOMMY JONES
RON HAMMING
JOEL FRITSCHE

"TAKING YOU FOR A RIDE SINCE 1955"

CASTLE BUILDERS
IF YOU CAN DREAM IT
WE CAN DO IT
STEVE MILLER JOHN OLSON SCOTT MILLER
MARCUS KING STEVE BOROWITZ
FIELD SUPERINTENDENTS

STEVE MILLER is Senior Vice President of Sourcing and Procurement and Facility Services and Support at The Walt Disney Company.

JOHN OLSON spent 37 years with Walt Disney Imagineering as a designer and field art director, working on all Disney Parks worldwide.

SCOTT MILLER worked for Disney Development Company, the real-estate division of The Walt Disney Company.

MARCUS KING started in Imagineering in 1997 as a senior program manager. He became Principal Design and Production Manager in 2001, and then Director of Design and Production for Hong Kong Disneyland.

STEVE BOROWITZ was a scenic artist with Imagineering who specialized in aging, graining and marbling. He was also proficient at simulating brickwork, rock, and wood.

THE PALM READERS
"EVERY LINE TELLS A STORY"
FRANK CASSIN DOUG HARLOW
CRAIG HELLER DAVID HARDING
DELINEATORS

FRANK CASSIN is Director of Estimating and Project Controls Manager for Domestic and International Resort Development.

DOUGLAS HARLOW is Director of Project Estimating at Imagineering.

CRAIG HELLER was a project estimator at Imagineering.

DAVID A. HARDING is Principal Project Estimator at Imagineering.

Exotic Specimens
Flower St. Nursery
Paul Comstock   John Sorenson
"We're Always Growing"

Paul Comstock contributed to the landscape of Disneyland Paris. He was promoted to Chief Landscape Architect and Designer of Disney's Animal Kingdom before it opened in 1998. He later became Director of Landscape Design for Hong Kong Disneyland.

John Sorenson is Director of Landscape and Architecture for Imagineering.

Chamber of Commerce
"Boosting Main Street Since 1871"
Irene Chan   Roy Hardy   Greg Wann   Larry Wilk
Board of Directors

Irene Chan was Regional Director of Corporate Communications for The Walt Disney Company for the Asia Pacific Region, before becoming Vice President of Public Affairs for Hong Kong Disneyland.

Roy Tan Hardy was originally a marketing strategist for The Walt Disney Company. He became Vice President of Marketing and Sales before becoming Senior Vice President of Marketing and Sales for Hong Kong Disneyland.

Greg Wann is Vice President of Human Resources at Hong Kong Disneyland.

Larry Wilk was Vice President of Business Design and Development for Disneyland Resort from 1994 until 2001. He became Vice President of Operations Services at Hong Kong Disneyland until 2006. He was promoted to Vice President of Operations and Strategy and Worldwide Operations, a role he inhabited until leaving the Company in 2013.

Main St. Supply Co.
"If You Need It, We Supply It"
Alex Boen Noble Coker Brian T. Jones Klaus Mager
Where Quality Is In Good Supply

Alexander Boen is Director of Costuming for Imagineering.

Noble Coker was Director of Information Technology for Hong Kong Disneyland. In 2005, he was promoted to Vice President and Chief Information Officer. Now, he is Vice President of Operations for the entire resort.

Brian T. Jones started as a ride and show engineer at Walt Disney World in 1989. He became Manager of Engineering Services from 1997 until 2002, when he became Director of Facility Services for Hong Kong Disneyland. He returned to Walt Disney World in 2006, where he became Director of Manufacturing, then Director of Engineering Services, and now serves as Director of Reedy Creek Energy Services.

Klaus Mager was Resident Manager of the Disneyland Hotel at Disneyland Resort from 1986 until 1995, when he became Director of Food and Beverage for the resort. He relocated in 2001 to become Director of Food and Beverage for Hong Kong Disneyland.

ORIGINAL STAFFING SERVICES
"WE HIRE THE BEST...& TRAIN THE REST"
BILL ERNEST   MANAGER
ANDREW BOLSTEIN   CURT SANDERS   BRYAN WONG
ASSOCIATES

BILL ERNEST joined Disney in 1994 as General Manager of Disney's Hilton Head Island Resort in South Carolina. He became General Manager of Field Business and then General Manager for many of Walt Disney World's Resorts. He went on to become Managing Director of Operations at Hong Kong Disneyland before being promoted to Executive Vice President and Managing Director of the Resort. He now serves as President and Managing Director for Asia for Walt Disney Parks and Resorts.

ANDREW BOLSTEIN became Manager of Industrial Engineering at Walt Disney World in 1995. In 2000, he became Director of Park Operations and Industrial Engineering for Hong Kong Disneyland. He is now Vice President of Trip Operations for Adventures by Disney.

CURT SANDERS was Manager of Operations Development for Disneyland Paris from 1987 until 1992. He then served a year as Director of Operations Development for Disney California Adventure. From 2001 until 2005, he was Director of Resort Development for Hong Kong Disneyland. He now serves as Director of Resort Development for Disneyland Resort.

BRYAN WONG was Manager of Business Planning and Development for Hong Kong Disneyland from 2000 until 2002. He was promoted to Director of Operations Services, a role he kept until leaving the Company in 2008.

THE ORIGINAL ENGINEERS
NEW STRUCTURES & OLD LIFTS
MIKE MCCULLOUGH   DAVE DOW

MIKE MCCULLOUGH is Vice President of Environmental Design and Engineering for Imagineering.

DAVE DOW was Manager of Electrical Engineering for Imagineering from 1987 until 1998. Then he became Director of Facility Engineering for four years, before becoming Director of Imagineering until 2002.

Town Square Planning Company
"No Land Too Big for Our Big Ideas"
Tom Morris
Chris Carradine
Surveyors

Tom Morris was Show Producer for Fantasyland at Disneyland Paris, and would later become Vice President and Executive Producer of Hong Kong Disneyland.

Chris Carradine was Vice President and Executive Concept Architect for Hong Kong Disneyland.

Art Henderson
Ed Erlandson
David Brickey
Chris Barker
Insiders and Outsiders
Design & Build Company

Art Henderson was an engineer at Imagineering.

Edward "Ed" Erlandson is Director of Architecture and Engineering at The Walt Disney Company.

David Brickey is Director of Interior Design at The Walt Disney Company.

Christopher N. Barker is Director of Graphic Design at The Walt Disney Company.

Creative Contractors Inc.
"We Manage To Get It Done"
Howard Brown   Randy Kalish   Doug LeBlanc
Dev Hawley   Ian Price
Designers' Representatives

Howard Brown was Executive Director of Hong Kong Disneyland. He went on to become Vice President of Creative and Project Development for Imagineering.

Randy Kalish was Vice President and Executive Director of Imagineering.

Doug LeBlanc was Vice President of Project Management for Hong Kong Disneyland.

Dev Hawley was Senior Development Manager for Hong Kong Disneyland.

Ian Price started with Disney in 1987 as the purchasing manager responsible for ride and show contracts. He was promoted to Project Director for Discoveryland in Disneyland Paris before taking on his current role of Director of Project Management for Imagineering for Hong Kong Disneyland.

Lock and Key Hospitality Co.
Our Rooms are Your Castle
Bob Holland   Jeremy Chaston   Gary Hasell
Jim Kwasnowski   Joe Haughney   Robert Ren
Owner's Representatives

Robert J. "Bob" Holland was Senior Project Engineer and Chief Architectural Engineer for Walt Disney World from 1979 through 1984. He was promoted to Manager of Design, and stayed in that position until 1986, when he became Vice President of Disney Development. He left the Company in 2006.

JEREMY CHASTON is Vice President of Construction Management for The Walt Disney Company.

GARY HASELL is Executive Director and Principal Architect at Imagineering.

JIM KWASNOWSKI was a project manager for Hong Kong Disneyland. He is now Vice President of Real Estate Development for The Walt Disney Company.

JOE HAUGHNEY was a project manager for Hong Kong Disneyland.

ROBERT REN was a project manager for Hong Kong Disneyland.

WDI School of Management
We Make Business A Pleasure
Don Goodman Headmaster
Jim Thomas & John Verity
Professors of Business Practices & Field Services

Don Goodman was President of Imagineering during the construction of Hong Kong Disneyland, and went on to become Senior Vice President of Disney Resort Real Estate.

Jim Thomas is Senior Vice President of Project Management at Imagineering.

John Verity was Project Manager for Frontierland at Disneyland Paris, Managing Director of Walt Disney Imagineering Hong Kong, and now serves as a project management Vice President of Imagineering.

Far East Development Co.
We bring Magic to the World
Jay Rasulo Home Office Manager
Wing Chao Traveling Representative

Jay Rasulo was Chairman of Walt Disney Parks and Resorts. He is currently Senior Executive Vice President, and Chief Financial Officer.

Wing T. Chao was Vice Chairman of Asia Pacific Development of Walt Disney Parks and Resorts, and Executive Vice President of Imagineering.

SAFE & SECURE INVESTMENT CO.
"OUR CONTROLS ARE UNDER CONTROL"
ANDY BERST
MARIAM IM
PHILIP YEUNG
COUNSELORS

ANDY BERST was Director of Finance for Walt Disney World from 1993 until 2007. From 2003, he also served as Director of Walt Disney Parks and Resorts.

MARIAM IM was Director of Financial Management and Treasury for The Walt Disney Company for Hong Kong Disneyland.

PHILIP YEUNG worked in the finance department for Hong Kong Disneyland.

Theatrical Agency
Bringing Broadway Magic to Asia's Avenues
Talent Agents
Anne Hamburger
Roger Heartsner
Laurie Jordan
"We Will Act On Your Behalf."

Anne Hamburger was Executive Vice President of Walt Disney Creative Entertainment from 2000 until 2008.

Roger Heartsner was a project director for the live shows at Hong Kong Disneyland.

Laurie Jordan worked with Anne Hamburger to help develop the live shows at Hong Kong Disneyland. She was Vice President of the Entertainment and Costuming Department. In the original version of the window, her name was misspelled as Lanrie.

Blank Sheet Paper Co.
"We Make the First Mark"
Marty Sklar & Tom Fitzgerald
"Dedicated to Making it Write"

Martin A. "Marty" Sklar joined WED Enterprises in 1961 to work on the attractions for the 1964-1965 New York World's Fair. In 1974, Marty became Creative Lead of Imagineering, and helped develop Disney theme parks around the world for the next 35 years.

Tom Fitzgerald wanted to be an Imagineer ever since he attended the 1964-1965 New York World's Fair as a child. Eventually, he became Executive Vice President of Story, Script and Media for Theme Park Productions, who are in charge of all film projects for the Parks. In 2001, he was promoted to Executive Vice President and Senior Creative Executive for Imagineering. He is also known as being the model for the submarine-repairing boyfriend in Horizons.

Established 1855
City of Main Street
Don Robinson
City Manager
Carl Williams
Treasurer

DON ROBINSON was Executive Vice President and Group Managing Director for Hong Kong Disneyland.

CARL WILLIAMS was Senior Vice President and Chief Financial Officer for Hong Kong Disneyland.

Hong Kong Disneyland
Casting Agency
Open Since '05
"It Takes People to Make the Dream a Reality"

This Window is a tribute to all Hong Kong Disneyland Resort Cast Members, past and present. It is the one "Casting Agency" Window that does not have Walt's name on it.

Flower St. Theater Co.
Dramas Musicals
Operas & Other Theatricals

Flower St. Theater Company is a reference to 1401 Flower Street, where Walt Disney Imagineering is located in Glendale, California.

Disney Bros. Studio

Disney Brothers Studio was the name of the studio Walt and Roy used for their first cartoons.

DANCE STUDIO OF ORLANDO
LESSONS FROM
BALLET TO BALLROOM

DANCE STUDIO OF ORLANDO refers to the fact that most of the performers for the shows and parades were trained by Cast Members from Walt Disney World in Orlando, Florida.

BURBANK BOOKKEEPING
"LET US TAKE A LOOK
AT YOUR LEDGERS"

BURBANK BOOKKEEPING refers to Burbank, California where the bookkeeping for the Park was done.

PAUL McAVITY, D.D.S.
DENTISTS IN TRAINING

PAUL McAVITY is not a real person, but a play on words for "pull my cavity."

MARCELINE MUSIC
PIANO, FLUTE, HARP, VOICE
LESSONS AVAILABLE

MARCELINE MUSIC is a reference to Marceline, Missouri where Walt spent some of his formative years.

GRAND CENTRAL
REAL ESTATE CO.
HOUSES
BOUGHT & SOLD

GRAND CENTRAL AIR TERMINAL was originally an airport in Glendale, California, that was used until 1959. The Walt Disney Company bought it in 1997, and it is the current home of Walt Disney Imagineering. If you look at some of the photos behind the glass, you'll see that one of them is of the Chicago home that Walt Disney was born in.

LAW OFFICES
NO CONTRACTS TOO COMPLEX OR TOO COMPLETE
PETER STEINMAN
TONY BASALARI
BETTY CHOI
INTERPRETERS

PETER E. STEINMAN is Deputy Chief Counsel and Head of Legal at Imagineering.

ANTHONY "TONY" BASALARI was Associate General Counsel at the time of Hong Kong Disneyland's construction. He is now Senior Vice President of Counsel at the Legal Department of Imagineering.

BETTY CHOI was Senior Vice President of Regional Counsel when Hong Kong Disneyland was under construction. She is now Chief Counsel for Asia Parks and Resorts for Disney.

GENERAL SUPPLIERS
"IF IT EXISTS,
WE CAN FIND IT"
"IF WE DON'T HAVE IT,
IT DOESN'T EXIST"
JIM CARLSON
STEWART ROBERTSON
ALASTAIR STIRLING

JIM CARLSON was Director of Project Planning, and Director of Scheduling and Integration for The Walt Disney Company.

STEWART ROBERTSON was Director of Sourcing and Procurement for The Walt Disney Company.

ALASTAIR STIRLING was Director of Quantity Surveying for Hong Kong Disneyland.

GLA Real Estate
Parcels Bought Sold and Leased
Improvements Upon Request
Angus Cheng
Chris Crary
Tony Killeen
John Lindsay
Agents

Angus Cheng started working for Disney in 1990 as Development Manager for Disneyland Paris. In 2001, he became Director of Development for the construction of Hong Kong Disneyland.

Chris Crary was Director of Planning and Architecture for Imagineering during Hong Kong Disneyland's construction.

Tony Killeen has been Director of Environmental Design and Engineering for Imagineering since 1998.

John Lindsay was Vice President of Project Management before becoming Vice President of Imagineering.

"Our Business Is Building"
The Construction Corporation
"If We Build It, They Will Come"
Jerre Kirk   Paul La France

Jerre Kirk was a senior project estimator at Imagineering from 1989 until 1992, when he became Principal Project Estimator. He stayed in that position until 1996, when he was promoted to Principal Construction Manager. In 1998, he took over as Director of Construction for Imagineering, a position he still holds today.

Paul La France was Project Director for Adventureland at Disneyland Paris. He was Head of Design and Construction for Walt Disney Studios Park, and Head of Construction of Hong Kong Disneyland. Before leaving Disney, he was Project Vice President of Imagineering.

Photo Credits

Disneyland Photos by Sarah Vincent

Magic Kingdom Photos by Norman Gidney
See more of Norman's work at:
www.MiceChat.com

Tokyo Disneyland Photos and Hong Kong Disneyland Photos by
Daniel Wanderman
See more of Daniel's work at:
www.Instagram.com/DanielWanderman

Disneyland Paris Photos by Hugh Allison and Todd West
See more of Todd's work at:
www.DisneyParksEarchive.com

ACKNOWLEDGMENTS

THIS BOOK WAS a monumental task, and if it wasn't for the help of the following folks, it would have never gotten done:

First and foremost, a big thank you to Sarah Vincent, Norm Gidney, Todd West, Hugh Allison, and Daniel Wanderman for their photos of the Windows. Even though some of the Parks are right in my backyard, their photographic skills captured them better than I ever could. And when I couldn't travel to the more exotic Parks, they brought back the Windows, in photographic form, to help me with my research.

Also, a huge thank you to the many folks who helped me research the names that I had difficulty with, reaching into their mind palaces (or massive archives) to help me out. Those folks include Hugh Allison, Bob Gurr, Rolly Crump, Chuck Snyder, David Todd, Eddie Sotto, Jeff Burke, Dave Smith, and Bill Sullivan.

Thank you to Justin Scarred, Matt Bateman, Dakota Bradford, Johnathen Hopkins, Hugh Allison, Todd West, Lisa Lincoln, and Johnny Lincoln who helped with checking the order of the Windows and ensuring none were missed.

Thank you to Emma Leavitt for her amazing cover art and backgrounds.

Hugh Allison deserves an extra shout-out for being one hell of an editor.

A big thank you to the folks at Orchard Hill Press for believing in this book and helping make it a reality.

Of course, friends are what keep you going, and without the support of George Taylor and Keith Gluck, I would have had no one pestering me to get this done.

Speaking of friends, thank you to Benjamin Shrader, Zak Borovay, Russell Flores, Estelle Hallick, and Kolby Ratigan for pre-reading and offering their advice.

Last, but certainly not least, to my love, Martina Gona, for always supporting me in everything I do.